PARALLEL MOVEMENT

OF THE HANDS

ALSO BY JOHN ASHBERY

POETRY

Turandot and Other Poems

Some Trees

The Tennis Court Oath

Rivers and Mountains

The Double Dream of Spring

Three Poems

The Vermont Notebook

Self-Portrait in a Convex Mirror

Houseboat Days

As We Know

Shadow Train

A Wave

Selected Poems

April Galleons

Flow Chart

Hotel Lautréamont

And the Stars Were Shining

Can You Hear, Bird

Wakefulness

The Mooring of Starting Out:
The First Five Books of Poetry

Girls on the Run

Your Name Here

As Umbrellas Follow Rain

Chinese Whispers

Where Shall I Wander

A Worldly Country

Notes from the Air: Selected Later Poems

Collected Poems, 1956–1987

Collected Poems, 1991–2000

Planisphere

Quick Question

Breezeway

Commotion of the Birds

FICTION

A Nest of Ninnies (with James Schuyler)

PLAYS

Three Plays

CRITICISM AND ESSAYS

Reported Sightings: Art Chronicles, 1957–1987

Other Traditions (The Charles Eliot Norton Lectures)

Selected Prose

PARALLEL
MOVEMENT

OF THE

HANDS

FIVE UNFINISHED LONGER WORKS

JOHN
ASHBERY

EDITED BY

EMILY SKILLINGS

AND WITH A FOREWORD

BY BEN LERNER

An Imprint of HarperCollinsPublishers

THIS BOOK IS DEDICATED TO

DAVID KERMANI

AND TO THE MEMORY OF

J A

CONTENTS

Foreword: Never Finished **XI**

Introduction **XV**

THE HISTORY OF PHOTOGRAPHY
7

THE ART OF FINGER DEXTERITY

1. Application of the Fingers with Quiet Hand **47**

2. The Passing of the Thumb **48**

3. Clarity in Velocity **49**

4. Light Articulation in Half-Staccato **50**

5. Evenness in Double Runs **51**

6. Clarity in Broken Chords **52**

7. Changing Fingers on the Same Key **53**

8. Light Articulation of the Left Hand **54**

9. Delicacy in Skips and Staccatos **56**

10. Exercise for Thirds [I] **57**

Exercise for Thirds [II] **58**

11. Skill in Alternating Fingers **59**

12. Flexibility of the Left Hand **60**

13. Maximum Velocity **6 1**

14. Chord Passages **6 3**

15. Wide Position in Fortissimo **6 4**

16. Alternating Fingers at Speed **6 5**

17. Minor Scales at High Speed **6 6**

18. Crossing the Hands Naturally and with a Fine Touch **6 7**

19. Tense Positions with a "Peaceful" Wrist **6 8**

20. Double Octaves **6 9**

21. Parallel Movement of the Hands [I] **7 0**

Parallel Movement of the Hands [II] **7 2**

22. Exercise for the Trill **7 4**

23. Light Touch of the Left Hand **7 6**

24. The Thumb on the Black Keys
with the Hand Absolutely Quiet **7 7**

25. Agility and Clarity **7 9**

26. Maximum Velocity in Arpeggios **8 0**

SACRED AND PROFANE DANCES

Attainder **8 5**

Sacred and Profane Dances **9 0**

Tempest **9 3**

21 VARIATIONS ON MY ROOM

9 9

THE KANE RICHMOND PROJECT

Spy Smasher 117

Perils of Nyoka 119

The Devil Diamond 119

The Lost City 121

Racing Blood 122

A Hard Man 132

The President's Dream 132

[untitled] "Kane was a righteous dude, heat-packing" 133

Chapter Seven 136

The Mist Rolls in from the Sea 137

Dog Overboard! 139

Dog and Pony Show 139

A Lost Dog 140

My Own Best Customer 141

Dog of the Limberlost 147

Sex on the River 148

A Long and Sleepy History 150

The Quitter 156

More about Drew 157

Modern Sketch 158

To Meet with My Father 161

[untitled] "I liked the fourth declension—all those 'u's" 1 6 2

Miss Otis Regrets Land's End 1 6 3

[untitled] "Are you trying to stop us?" 1 6 4

[untitled] "Nothing if found convenient" 1 6 6

There You Go! 1 6 7

[untitled] "Why wait for another day to cross itself?" 1 7 0

Arguably, 1 7 3

An Unspecified Amount 1 7 4

très modéré 1 7 5

Fried Mackerel and Frozen Peas 1 7 6

[untitled] "The point is to find an
extra-sensual way to be without it" 1 7 7

Dates and Entries 1 8 7

Appendix A: The History of Photography 1 9 9

Appendix B: The Art of Finger Dexterity 2 1 1

Appendix C: Sacred and Profane Dances 2 1 9

Appendix D: 21 Variations on My Room 2 2 5

Appendix E: The Kane Richmond Project 2 2 9

Acknowledgments 2 6 3

NEVER FINISHED

In 1971, John Ashbery read from his great prose poem, "The System," at St. Mark's Poetry Project on the Lower East Side of Manhattan. Arriving at the podium, Ashbery realized he'd misplaced the ending of the poem:

> Oh. I don't think I have the last page of it with me. Well, it doesn't really matter, actually … I do like the way it ends, but it's kind of an environmental work, if I may be so bold. If you sort of feel like leaving at any point, it won't really matter. You will have had the experience … I am disturbed that it's incomplete, but maybe that's good.

"The System," with its vast paragraphs of cascading sentences, is no doubt more of an "environmental work" than most of Ashbery's poetry, but his suspicion of closure, his openness to incompletion, are well documented across his writing and conversation. "For to be finished / is nothing," Ashbery writes in "The History of Photography," the most finished of the unfinished poems in this volume, the first book of Ashbery's poetry to appear since his death in 2017. "Only children and dinosaurs like endings / and we shall all be very happy once it gets broken off."

In Ashbery's writing, mentions of artistic "finish"—varnish, polish, completion—usually evoke death, how time finishes *us* off. In his "Self-Portrait in a Convex Mirror," for example, a poem first published in 1974, aesthetic finish is the enemy of living art: "The picture is almost finished, / The surprise almost over …"; Parmigianino's finish is "enigmatic," but also "bland"; and the artist's remarkable "Secrets of wash and finish that took a lifetime / To learn" are "reduced to the status of / Black-and-white illustrations in a book where colorplates / Are rare." To be finished is to be fixed and already fading, a museum piece, a dinosaur, but that's not the fate of all artworks, all poems; poetry can also be a machine for suspending time. In a John Ashbery poem—and especially in his long poems, which, until this book, I'd wrongly believed he'd stopped writing at some point in the late 1990s—we don't just decipher meanings the poet deposited in the past. Instead, we set the machinery of meaning-making into motion each time we read, each time we enter the poem's environment in the present tense. Maybe this is true of all great writing, but it's particularly true of Ashbery's. Even when one of his poems ends beautifully (and I believe Ashbery composed some of the finest endings in English), it nevertheless breaks off—a circuit is broken when we look up from the page. The experience, however, is endlessly renewable; we just have to recharge the poem with our attention in order to encounter afresh the waveform action of syntax, the making and unmaking of sense, the how, not the what, of knowing. From "Flexibility of the Left Hand":

> We were finished and knew it, but like as not we didn't know it and were unfinished, a work of art. That and so much else. Calmly we note that here. It is merry. Yet the tide comes in on precise steps and that is to be how we know.

Unlike others of its kind, the book you're holding is, in fact, merry. Posthumous volumes are typically lugubrious affairs—collections of the poems death cut short, false starts perhaps better left unseen. But "unfinished" is a term of praise for Ashbery, a term of art. The Ashbery poem, no matter how carefully composed, revised, has to be left a little unrealized, open to the participation of future readers; that's how it cheats death. I'm not saying these five works lovingly assembled by Emily Skillings are better for never having been completed—Ashbery strove to perfect his machines for defeating time and he made clear which poems he thought were failures—but it feels right (and light and moving) that the first volume to appear since his passing is made up of poems still in process, poems in which the resistance to finish is itself a unifying theme. It makes this book a "hymn to possibility," to borrow a phrase Ashbery used when reviewing Gertrude Stein in 1957, a hymn to ongoingness, to the fluctuations of the Ashberian experience, instead of a work of mourning. His poems refuse, like the Hollywood serials he celebrates in *The Kane Richmond Project*, to end, to remain ended:

> Then he's going to put in that wonderful girl at the end
> and the book will be finished, though not the sequel,
> or a second or a third if the demand arises.

Reviewing Marianne Moore's *Complete Poems* in the *New York Times* in 1967—her complete poems followed her collected poems—Ashbery praised Moore's endless revisions, her sequels, and looked forward to a "*More Complete Poems*": "as long as we can ask, like the student in her poem of that title, 'When will your experiment be finished,' we may expect the reply, 'Science is never finished.'" Ashbery didn't endlessly rework his poems as Moore did, but he did repurpose his own lines (one of the many fascinating aspects of Ashbery's process that Skillings illuminates in her excellent introduction and annotations), and his genius for deferral ensures that his poems, too, are "never finished"; they never take their place in the past, but instead invite us into their perpetual present. Ashbery is American poetry's Scheherazade, and in the poem "Scheherazade," written around the time of the "Self-Portrait," Ashbery describes: "A pleasant wavering of the air / In which all things seem present, whether / Just past or soon to come. It was all invitation." It was and it is. There is no last page to the poetry of John Ashbery. You will have had the experience; you can always have it again.

BEN LERNER

INTRODUCTION

*Look at how a pond reflects trees—imperfectly, perhaps, yet as perfectly as
it knows how, and the little mistakes in the reflection are what makes it
charming and nice, gives stealth to what would otherwise be a random
picture of choice. Surely this is the reason we are all drawn to art, and why
art loves us, and if anything were any different, that is more or less perfect,
it wouldn't have the same hold over us. What I mean is we can dream
safely in our environment because art has set soft, invisible limits to it.*

—JOHN ASHBERY, *The Kane Richmond Project*

The first time I met John Ashbery, I didn't see him. It was the summer
of 2010. I was twenty-one, just out of college, and had come to inter-
view for a job as his assistant. Ashbery's apartment was on the ninth
floor of a white-brick high-rise on the corner of Ninth Avenue and
22nd Street in Chelsea. I'd later learn that Ashbery and his husband,
David Kermani, had lived in this building, both separately and to-
gether, since the 1970s.

As I waited for the interview to begin, I admired a small collection
of black-and-white ceramic objects on a lacquered wooden table in the
apartment's entryway: a striped, gourdlike vase; a bud vase in the shape
of a row of three dice; and an oval box resembling a miniature covered
casserole dish. Individually, the pieces were beautiful and possessed
innate charms of shape, pattern, and representation; but placed near
one another, they took on a new energy, an importance of association.

Kermani showed me to a small office off the front hallway. As we sat down, he informed me that I wouldn't see Mr. Ashbery that day, since he was hard at work finishing the preface to his translation of Arthur Rimbaud's *Illuminations*. As Kermani and I discussed the details of the job, I could hear the percussive strikes of Ashbery's typewriter from the other side of the apartment. I received word later that week that, if I wished, I could be the assistant to my favorite poet. I occupied that position from 2010 until Ashbery's death in 2017.

The preface Ashbery was writing that day would come to hold a special resonance for me, as both the text that marked our first "meeting," and the first place where I encountered a definition of modern poetry that felt memorable, satisfying, and true. Ashbery writes the following of Rimbaud's *Illuminations*—prose poems that, for him, constituted the "fertile destabilization"[1] that makes a work modern: "absolute modernity was for [Rimbaud] the acknowledging of the simultaneity of all of life, the condition that nourishes poetry at every second.... If we are absolutely modern—and we are—it's because Rimbaud commanded us to be."[2] I remember thinking that this was also an accurate description of Ashbery's work and legacy—this enriching, unsettling simultaneity that opens up new possibilities in poetry and art.

In his unpublished manuscript *The Kane Richmond Project* (a title I italicize here in my belief that it could well have become a book-length poem), Ashbery writes,

---

1. John Ashbery, preface to *Illuminations*, Arthur Rimbaud, trans. Ashbery. W. W. Norton, 2011, 16.

2. Ibid.

> I listened to it on the radio
> wondering why nothing stops the serial
> free to go on inventing itself
> through fire through thunder through blisters of time
> and the world. Nothing much comes to cheat us
> of this vapor.[3]

In response to Ashbery's inquiry about the inevitable progression of the serial, I might ask, "What stops a poem?" All five manuscripts included in this collection contain an element of seriality: they are both divided and united by means of numbered and titled sections—unfolding as part of a larger architecture—all propelling them (and us, as readers) forward, toward some end, a final work; and yet, these works were halted, for one reason or another, along various stages of the production line. Readers and critics may have assumed that Ashbery's practice of long-form writing—which has always been an important element of his oeuvre—ended in 1999 with the publication of his book-length ekphrastic poem, *Girls on the Run*. In bringing these poems and projects together, it is my hope that they might, in addition to their intrinsic merits, illuminate some aspects of Ashbery's process, particularly his continuation of a long-form, project-based writing practice late into his career.

Written primarily between the early 1990s and the mid-aughts, the unfinished poems collected here indicate the variousness of Ashbery's writing—a set of wildly different experiments. Just as there is a spectrum of "finishedness" to these five works, there are also differences

---

3. *Parallel Movement of the Hands*, 148.

of scale and scope. Two of the projects, *The Art of Finger Dexterity* and *The Kane Richmond Project*, approach book length, and the remaining three, "The History of Photography," "Sacred and Profane Dances," and "21 Variations on My Room," are long poems or linked series.

I came across *The Kane Richmond Project* and *The Art of Finger Dexterity* in New York City in June 2018, while packing Ashbery's correspondence, original typescripts, and other collected papers into dozens of storage boxes for acquisition by Harvard University's Houghton Library. I didn't discover them by any means, as Kermani, Ashbery's biographer Karin Roffman, and other close friends were aware of their existence.[4] In fact, flipping through both published and unpublished manuscript materials (everything impeccably organized by Kermani), I was surprised to encounter my own handwriting on the tab of a manila folder. I hadn't recalled, until that moment, creating a folder for photocopies of Ashbery's unfinished manuscript based on the instructional compositions of Carl Czerny. As I read the beautiful poems inside, it occurred to me that others may like to see them, too. When I noticed the manuscript for *The Kane Richmond Project* nearby (toward the front of a file cabinet in an area reserved for ongoing projects), the idea for a collection of unfinished longer works began to grow.

In the years I worked for him, Ashbery wrote poetry several times

---

4. In the edited transcript of an unpublished 2015 interview with curator and art historian Hans Ulrich Obrist, Obrist asks Ashbery if he has any unfinished projects. Kermani, who was in the room during the interview, mentions both the Czerny-related manuscript materials and *The Kane Richmond Project*, as well as another unfinished poem, "For Leopardi, or Tolstoi," adding that he and I had been encouraging Ashbery to publish poems from *The Art of Finger Dexterity*, then referred to as the *Czerny Variations*.

per week; during certain periods, he did so nearly every day. This prolificacy slowed somewhat as his health declined or if he was involved with other projects that required his attention, but he continued writing regularly and making collages until the end of his life. His final poem, "Climate Correction," was written by hand at home in Hudson, New York, on August 25, 2017, a little more than a week before his death at age ninety. Because of this abundance, there are enough exceptional unpublished and uncollected Ashbery poems—even from the last twenty years—from which to create several collections. Both the 2008 and 2017 Library of America volumes, edited by Mark Ford, have included extensive previously uncollected material. The file cabinet contained many uncollected shorter poems that had not made their way into Ashbery's recent books. These included a grouping of poems written after the 2016 publication of *Commotion of the Birds*, many of which appeared in either anthologies or periodicals. Given all the finished poems that remain uncollected, one might reasonably ask, why my excitement at the prospect of a book of longer unfinished works? The first answer is the pleasure of reading these poems, but this volume is further justified by an aspect of Ashbery's process that I observed closely during my time as his assistant.

I was present for the writing and construction of Ashbery's three final collections, *Quick Question*, *Breezeway*, and *Commotion of the Birds*, and over the course of these three books, I watched a unique process unfold. When he had amassed a satisfactory quantity of poems—and before the work of ordering them began—he had the typescripts printed and put together into a folder. Ashbery would then do something that, when I first noticed it, startled me: He would read through the poems and grade them. Individual poems received markings of A,

B, and C; I never saw any D or F poems, though they may exist. Ashbery's opinion of his own work shifted quickly, and a poem that was an A on Tuesday could be downgraded to a B or even a C by Friday. Conversely, a poem he didn't initially care for could suddenly reveal to him its hidden pockets of brilliance. (Any poem or false start that Ashbery did not wish to be published would be boldly crossed out.) On occasion, he would even outsource this job: One of his favorite longtime substitute graders was poet and critic John Yau, Ashbery's friend and former student, who would receive a manuscript in the mail with instructions to grade the poems. Yau told me that Ashbery liked the way Yau challenged his perceptions of his own poetry. This appreciation, of course, had exceptions. Once, when Yau gave a B+ to a poem, Ashbery asked what prevented it from being an A, as he rather liked the poem and wanted to dispute the grade. When Yau pointed out a line he didn't care for and asked Ashbery what it meant, Ashbery responded, "That's something I learned my freshman year of college in a literature class!"[5]

At first, this grading process seemed antithetical to Ashbery's sensibility as a poet. How could a writer who so exemplified freedom and experimentation treat his poems the way a punitive teacher of creative writing might? Indeed, Ashbery, who taught poetry at Brooklyn College in the 1970s and was later the Charles P. Stevenson Jr. Professor of Languages and Literature at Bard College, mentioned his distaste for grading student poets in a 1988 interview with John Tranter, where he asserted: "[T]hey shouldn't have to pass an examination because they're poets who are writing poetry, and I don't like the idea of grad-

---

5. John Yau, conversation with ES, Jan. 7, 2020.

ing poems."[6] Although Ashbery based his self-grading on the perceived strengths of the poems, it became clear the grades served other functions. He admitted to me, Kermani, and others that he was not looking to rid a collection of B poems. An A poem exhibited certain characteristics understood to mark a "good poem," but this combination of desirable elements could be too often repeated over the course of a single collection. Ashbery thought that a book needed a combination of A and B poems in order to be well-balanced and surprising. A poem graded B (one that is a little "off," unsettling, or puzzling) could lend a necessary *something* to the mix. For this reason, several A poems that felt too similar to other strong poems included in an evolving manuscript—even ones he had already published in periodicals—may have been cut eventually, while other poems that received lesser grades remained.

Notably, these folders full of graded poems—the material from which the book manuscript was culled—typically excluded works that didn't make it into previous collections, since Ashbery didn't consider those to be of a piece with the more recent work, (though he was known to reuse parts of older, unpublished poems in the creation of new ones). Ashbery's disinclination to look back to older poetry applied to his published work as well. In a 1980 interview with David Remnick (who was then an undergraduate student at Princeton), Ashbery admitted, "Heidegger says that to write a poem is to make a voyage of discovery. In the same way, I am always interested in my future poems rather than the ones which I've already written. The old ones really don't do

---

6. John Ashbery and John Tranter, "John Ashbery in Conversation with John Tranter," *Jacket 2, Jacket Magazine* (May 1988), jacketmagazine.com/02/jaiv1988.html.

anything for me."[7] Ashbery's friend, poet Adam Fitzgerald, reminded me of a rare moment when he included a finished older poem in a new collection: Late in the process of compiling his final book, before it even had a title, Ashbery found a previously unpublished poem, from circa 2007, called "Witness to Titans." He wanted to include this poem—but, since it was written almost a decade prior, he was afraid it would seem disjointed from the more recent work. Eventually, he overcame this anxiety, placing the poem first in the manuscript and retitling it "Commotion of the Birds"—which later became the title of the collection.

Both of these factors—the grading, the hesitancy to publish work excluded from recent collections—contributed to my evolving feeling that the first volume of Ashbery's poetry to be posthumously published should avoid material he may have omitted from previous books because it felt too repetitive of themes and tones already present in them. By contrast, these unfinished longer works, which upon my very first reading drew me into their intricately crafted worlds, felt like a new set of textures.

The Five Works

In selecting work for this book, I didn't scour Ashbery's archives for unpublished poetry. To the contrary, this collection, for the most part, reflects what was simply *around* (with the exception of "The History

---

7. John Ashbery and David Remnick, "John Ashbery in Conversation with David Remnick," *Bennington Review 4: Staying Alive* (Fall/Winter 2017): 79. Originally published in *Bennington Review 8* (Sep. 1980).

of Photography," which I found while conducting research in Ashbery and Kermani's basement in Hudson). Four of these poems were stored and kept just several yards from where Ashbery wrote poetry and correspondence, watched the nightly news and caught films on Turner Classic Movies, talked on the phone with friends, and read in his favorite armchair. Though these projects hadn't been prepared for publication (a process that usually included retyping "clean" copies that integrated Ashbery's corrections), they also hadn't been sent to the archives or put into storage. They may have been suspended—paused on their way toward inclusion in a book—but they hadn't been abandoned. They were lived with; they were living. In response to an email I wrote about the possible publication of *The Kane Richmond Project* and *The Art of Finger Dexterity*, Eugene Richie—one of Ashbery's closest friends, editor of his *Selected Prose*, and also a former assistant—wrote, "I remember John telling me about these two works. My sense was that he didn't publish them because they would not fit into full books he was doing. Not because he felt they weren't publishable."[8] In much the same way, Richie—who prepared the computer typescripts of "Sacred and Profane Dances" for possible inclusion in *Selected Prose*—explained that Ashbery did not feel those pieces of creative prose belonged within the scope of that collection, since the other selected prose works were nonfiction. Through these revelations, I began to see these manuscripts as seeking one another's company. They were a collection of misfit projects that—because of length, focus, or form—either were ineligible for inclusion in other collections or had not yet grown to the length where they could be published on

---

8. Eugene Richie, email to ES, Aug. 18, 2018.

their own. When I brought them together, I saw the many ways they were in conversation. I have not ordered them chronologically but rather by thinking about their affinities and forms.

The book begins with "The History of Photography," a long poem composed in 1993, around the time Ashbery was writing the poems that appeared in *And the Stars Were Shining*. A network of references to important figures (such as Eugène Atget, Francis Frith, Eadweard Muybridge, Thomas Eakins, and Robert Mapplethorpe), technologies, images, and advancements in both early and contemporary photography creates a scaffold for Ashbery's moving and playful lyricism:

> How could I have had such a good idea?
> But you know, the way they all say is a barrel.
> Times two and too much. I have been coming and going
> a fair share of my life, and some of me is up there,
> photographed. Like a chair listening to a victrola record
> I experience too little and know too much
> for the good of others and their bathing suits.
>
> Then too, as much escapes me as a tailor's dummy
> in a photograph by Atget, taking in everything and nothing,
> which caused the rain to fall one day.[9]

Reminiscent of the movement and scope of Ashbery's groundbreaking poem "Self-Portrait in a Convex Mirror," "The History of Photography" sets its sights not on a single artwork but on the historical advancements of a medium, allowing the poem's aperture to consider the role of the captured image in both personal and broader cultural terms.

---

9. *Parallel Movement of the Hands*, 8.

In Ashbery's unpublished poem "For Leopardi, or Tolstoi" (written June 1998)—which I found alongside *The Art of Finger Dexterity* and *The Kane Richmond Project* while packing away Ashbery's papers, and which I later discovered he "cannibalized" (his term for a process of self-quotation he often used when he was unhappy with a poem as a whole but fond of some of its components) and distributed throughout his collection *Your Name Here* (2000)[10]—he mentions the Austrian composer Carl Czerny: "I would prefer to be practicing my scales now; even the etudes of Czerny / would sound good in place of this brouhaha that bathes us, places its pawn // directly in front of the bishop." Czerny, a student of Beethoven and a teacher of Liszt, was the composer of nearly a thousand musical works. This impressive body of work included Op. 740, *The Art of Finger Dexterity*, which became the

---

10. *Your Name Here* production files, Hudson, NY. Courtesy of the Estate of John Ashbery. Intended for Ashbery's archive at Harvard University's Houghton Library, Cambridge, MA. Though I found this unfinished, seven-page poem in the section of the NYC filing cabinet dedicated to unfinished or ongoing projects, I ultimately decided not to include it in this collection, because it seemed to me Ashbery did with it exactly what he wanted—redistributing excerpts he liked into other poems, a common practice of his. John Shoptaw's *On the Outside Looking Out: John Ashbery's Poetry* (Harvard University Press, 1994) documents Ashbery's "recycling" of lines from his unpublished works in the construction of his poem "Fantasia on 'The Nut-Brown Maid'" (*Houseboat Days*, 1977), which Shoptaw describes as an "in-house collage" (214).

Six passages from "For Leopardi, or Tolstoi" were used in seven poems across *Your Name Here*: "Toy Symphony," "Poem on Several Occasions," "The File on Thelma Jordan," "*De Senectute*," "Our Leader Is Dreaming," "Strange Occupations," and "Another Aardvark." While looking through the *Your Name Here* production files, I found an additional poem, "Fires in the Creekbed," that was cut from the collection and which ends with the opening lines of "For Leopardi, or Tolstoi." "Fires in the Creekbed" appeared in *The Hat*, summer 2000.

blueprint for Ashbery's eponymous sequence, written in 2007.[11] Ashbery has always been influenced by music in his writing; many composers, including Elliott Carter, Alvin Lucier, Charles Wuorinen, Mark So, Robin Holloway, Ned Rorem, and Christian Wolff have collaborated with and responded to his poetry. On the topic of musical composition and its relationship to his poetry, Ashbery told pianist Sarah Rothenberg,

> composers do have ... the enviable task of writing in a language that cannot be argued with or even deciphered but which nevertheless has its meaning and its thrust. That's what I envy the most about composing, and I'm trying to do that in poetry, but unfortunately that's impossible, because everybody understands words, and the words have more or less the same meaning for everyone.[12]

Czerny's piece, in Ashbery's words, "was written to torture piano students. . . . It's mostly silly little tunes ornamented in a very complicated way to stretch the fingers to the limits of endurance. It's kind of beautiful because of having been written from that angle, to educate the fingers."[13] Ashbery, who remembered playing Czerny's *Études* while studying piano as a child,[14] completed poems titled after the first

---

11. For more information on Ashbery's title, see Appendix B.

12. John Ashbery and Sarah Rothenberg, "John Ashbery and Sarah Rothenberg: A Conversation on Music and Literature," The Ashbery Resource Center, The Flow Chart Foundation, www.flowchartfoundation.org/sarah-rothenberg. Courtesy of the Bard College Publications Office, 1992.

13. Nina Shengold, "Perennial Voyager: John Ashbery at Home," *Chronogram* [Hudson Valley Edition] (Sep. 2007): 57.

14. John Ashbery, unpublished interview with Hans Ulrich Obrist, Nov. 11, 2015, New York City. Transcript courtesy of the Estate of John Ashbery, Hudson, NY. Used with permission of interviewer.

twenty-six of the fifty variations that make up Op. 740. The titles "Parallel Movement of the Hands," and "Exercise for Thirds" are each used for two separate poems—a doubling pattern perhaps suggestive of hands moving alongside each other at the keyboard. Just as a piano student might practice Czerny's musical exercises, Ashbery returned to this manuscript diligently, writing twenty-eight poems in May, June, and July 2007.

"Sacred and Profane Dances" is an (as yet) undated grouping of prose poems, likely from much earlier in Ashbery's career. Its first two sections are a detailed commentary on the Parable of the Ten Virgins from the Gospel of Matthew, but its third section, "Tempest," seems to be a separate prose work, which was found together with the first two sections. I hadn't the heart to separate "Tempest" from its friends on account of its narrative nonconformity. Ashbery had an impressive collection of different versions of the Bible, including an old set of Bibles that had belonged to his family.[15] For a time, he was a subscriber to the Anchor Bible Commentary Series (a subset of the Anchor Bible Project), an ongoing serial publication in which new translations of the individual books of the Bible were annotated, contextualized, illustrated, and commented upon by various scholars.[16] In this unusual poem, Ashbery takes on the role of the biblical scholar, at times even taking the side of the silly virgins who have forgotten to add oil to their lamps, and provides interesting social commentary on the household at the center of this parable.

The shortest of the long poems in this collection, "21 Variations on My Room," written while Ashbery was taking a break from the longer,

---

15. David Kermani, conversation with ES, Nov. 11, 2019.
16. Ibid.

final poem in this book, *The Kane Richmond Project*, is interesting in relationship to this larger work. The two poems share a source text, common language, and even an epigraph, so there is a possibility that "21 Variations on My Room" was conceived as part of the larger project, though I have kept them separate for the purposes of this publication.

"Film has been a major influence on me. I think it's probably been more influential than visual art," Ashbery said in an interview with Daniel Kane.[17] In *The Glamorous Country*, an in-progress collection of essays on Ashbery and film, Yau notes, "John's taste in movies runs the gamut, from the high to the very bottom, and from obscure to popular. The terms 'tasteful' and 'tasteless' don't seem to apply, even as he watches forgotten films of the 1920s and '30s and forgettable films of the '50s and '60s."[18] This democratic viewing approach was something I witnessed while working with Ashbery, who—with his near-encyclopedic knowledge of even the most obscure films—was always finding ways to collapse lived experience with memories of and language from movies he'd seen. Ashbery chronicled his foundational relationship to film most famously in the prose poem "The Lonedale Operator," which begins, "The first movie I ever saw was the Walt Disney cartoon *The Three Little Pigs*. My grandmother took me to it. It was back in the days when you went 'downtown.'"[19] This poem, with its progression of film-related memories (names of actors, scenery, synopses, etc.), puts us simultaneously in the

---

17. Daniel Kane, "Reading John Ashbery's *The Tennis Court Oath* through Man Ray's Eye," *Textual Practice* 21, 3 (2007): 553.

18. John Yau, *The Glamorous Country*. Forthcoming. Used with permission of author.

19. John Ashbery, "The Lonedale Operator," *A Wave*, in *John Ashbery: Collected Poems, 1956–1987*, ed. Mark Ford. Library of America, 2008, 771.

seats of the audience and in the space of memory—linking the inherently cinematic experiences of remembering with the particular sensations, shocks, terrors, and revelations that occur when we take in a work of film. In his published poetry, Ashbery has carved out a special place for references to cinema, but he also mirrors the "technical processes" of film-making in his writing, as pointed out by Kermani's poignant essay "John Ashbery's Cinema Paradiso: Domestic Elements as Poetry."[20] Nowhere are the combinations and manifestations of these concepts more fully present than in this book's ambitious final manuscript, *The Kane Richmond Project*, written in 2002. Cutting between prose and lineated passages, this nearly forty-manuscript-page hybrid poem is a love letter to the antics of the serial form.

In the poem "The Phantom Agents," from *Hotel Lautréamont* (1992), Ashbery writes,

> we must seek the answer in decrepit cinemas
> whose balconies were walled off decades ago: on the screen
> (where, in posh suburbia, a woman waits),

---

20. "Understandably then, film has also been one of the most pervasive influences on his work, in ways ranging from the literal use of movie subject matter and references to the appropriation of technical processes. Memory is a key ingredient in this mix: film *in* memory, film *and* memory, film *as* memory. And because film may be the art form that can come closest to mirroring the way the human mind works, which itself is one of the primary concerns of Ashbery's work, an understanding of Ashbery's relationship with cinema is likely to be productive." David Kermani, "John Ashbery's Cinema Paradiso: Domestic Elements as Poetry," *A Dream of This Room: A Created Spaces Portfolio of Works on John Ashbery's Textual and Domestic Environments*, ed. Micaela Morrissette, 2008, www.rain taxi.com/literary-features/john-ashbery-created-spaces/john-ashberys-cinema-paradiso -domestic-elements-as-poetry/.

under the seats, in the fuzz and ancient vomit and gumwrappers;
or in the lobby, where yellowing lobby cards announce
the advent of next week's Republic serial: names
of a certain importance once, names that float
in the past, like a drift of gnats on a summer evening.[21]

The Kane Richmond Project revitalizes this space of the "decrepit" cinema and its forgotten names, taking as its narrative backdrop two Republic serials, both starring handsome actor Kane Richmond: *Spy Smasher* and *The Adventures of Rex and Rinty* (the latter costarring canine actor Rin Tin Tin Jr., aka "Rinty," who, along with horse "Rex," becomes another major player in the poem). The poem incorporates and commingles plotlines and character names from these serials, along with manifold references to other films from the 1920s, '30s, and '40s. *The Kane Richmond Project* also follows in the tradition of Ashbery's long poems "The Skaters" and "Europe" in the way that it uses literature written for children as a collage element, sourcing quotes from Tom Swift and Hardy Boys adventure novels. With its reappearing cast of characters, the poem feels very much connected to *Girls on the Run* (1999), typescripts and drafts of which I consulted closely while making structural and editorial decisions for *The Kane Richmond Project*.

21. John Ashbery, "The Phantom Agents," *Hotel Lautréamont*, in *John Ashbery: Collected Poems, 1991–2000*, ed. Mark Ford. Library of America, 2017, 238–39.

Always Becoming

One of the aspects of Ashbery's work that has both engaged and frustrated readers and critics is the way his poems leave room for the reader to make their own connections among images, gestures, and moments of intertextuality—a signature openness that has been nurtured by Ashbery's well-documented hesitancy (both in interviews and in his own writing) to comment upon the meaning of his work. Unfortunately, this *grande permission*—to borrow a phrase from Henri Michaux—has often been recast as Ashbery's "difficulty" or "inaccessibility." In my years reading Ashbery, I have often considered how I encounter this openness as a reader: I approach it with wonder and gratitude for the permission it has granted me, the participation it has asked of me. This quality of openness that I experience as a gift to the reader nonetheless presents certain challenges to the editor.

While transcribing *The Kane Richmond Project*, I encountered a typo in the manuscript's final pages that came to exemplify a particularly Ashberian conundrum.

> It may happen then as it has in the past that the spider king will unhitch himself to plummet directly into our daily affairs as they seemed on the point *ot hopening* [emphasis mine], creating themselves and us as a by-product?

I had two options to choose from: "of happening" and "of opening." "Opening," the word I selected because it seemed likelier, given both the organization of the keyboard and that the entire word is contained within the misspelling, fulfills the haunting image of the spider falling through the dilations in space and reality created by events. While I am confident in my choice, "affairs as they seemed on the point of happening" recalls art critic Jed Perl's description of Ashbery's way of seeing (or urging us to see) art in his criticism—and, I would argue, in his poetry as well:

> Ashbery always insists that we respond to art in many different ways, that art is *pictura* and *poesis* and philosophy as well, that we can discover the literary within the pictorial, the pictorial within the literary, and discover all of this to all sorts of varying degrees, in one part of a work of art, in a particular work of art at a particular time. The result is not anarchic, not in any way, but rather suggests that art is the disciplined exercise of a range of possibilities, with the work provoking branchings of thought and experience and feeling, all sorts of openings, analogies, echoings, doublings. Ashbery shows us that seeing, which provokes thinking, makes us see other things, which in turn enables us to think other things. This is an aesthetic that rejects fixed aesthetic distinctions, that is hybrid, impure, always evolving, for the artwork, as long as we are looking at it or thinking about it, is never fixed, is always becoming.[22]

This alternate phrasing, wherein events seem to be "on the point of happening," embodies the continually renewing precipice of experience in Ashbery's poetry, an "always becoming" that treats us to its diversions, distractions, and recalculations, its own perpetual regeneration and undoing. Even in the specific uncertainties presented by a not fully corrected manuscript, these unpublished works were "pro-

---

22. Jed Perl, "A Magically Alive Aesthetic," *Conjunctions*, John Ashbery Tribute, eds. Peter Gizzi and Bradford Morrow, 49 (2007): 371.

voking branchings of thought and experience and feeling." I encountered many such cruxes in the texts while editing, and I have tried to indicate them in the appendices whenever possible, explaining my choices while offering other possibilities. Perl's phrases "always evolving . . . never fixed . . . always becoming" also resonate with me in terms of the poet's process, as they challenge the idea of a final work. How could we see these works, in their various stages of completion, as fully realized in their own states of becoming?

Ashbery was a careful editor and reviser of his own poetry, especially when it came to longer projects, but his revision process was such that it rarely caused a draft to stray too far from the "original thought."[23] In the appendix to *On the Outside Looking Out*, an illuminating, in-depth critical companion to Ashbery's collections, from *Some Trees* through *Flow Chart*, John Shoptaw describes Ashbery's revision process for his long poem, "A Wave":

> Ashbery keeps to the original by keeping new writing to a minimum. Rather than changing the fabric of his text by rewriting or interpolating phrases and lines, Ashbery revises from the outside by cutting and restitching—scrapping what doesn't work and leaving the reconnected pieces relatively intact. . . . Thus Ashbery can revise heavily and still keep close to an, if not the, original.[24]

---

23. "I like the idea of being as close to the original thought or voice as possible and not to falsify it by editing," John Ashbery in Peter Stitt, "The Art of Poetry XXXIII: John Ashbery," *The Paris Review* 90 (Winter 1983): 58. Quoted in Shoptaw, *On the Outside Looking Out*, 343 (see note below).

24. John Shoptaw, "The Building of 'A Wave,'" appendix to *On the Outside Looking Out*. Harvard University Press, 1994, 343.

Seeing this process firsthand across these manuscripts—wherein the poem's original fabrication is kept close in the act of revision—further clarified my role in presenting these poems for the first time.

On April 13, 2000, Ashbery wrote a letter to his longtime, beloved editor Elisabeth Sifton at Farrar, Straus and Giroux, attached to a revised draft of his manuscript *Your Name Here*. He began: "Dear Elisabeth, Here is the ms. I know that copy editors prize consistency; as a poet, I don't; but I have tried to overcome this inexcusable trait in as many instances as possible."[25]

Sifton's same-day response—proof of her superb talent and generosity as an editor of poetry—includes a note that addresses Ashbery's description of a type of English rose, the Maréchal Niel, as "milk-pink" in his poem "The Green Dress," noting that this varietal is "usually pale yellow." She followed up later that week with a faxed, handwritten bouquet of "19th-century milk-pink French roses" for Ashbery to choose from, signed "your ob't rose servant." He eventually landed on Souvenir de la Malmaison, because Madame Alfred Carrière was already used by James Schuyler in a poem, and Ashbery worried that readers might confuse Fantin-Latour with the French painter after whom it is named.[26] Her letter also contains an interesting query about the title of his poem, "Cinéma Vérité": "I can't understand what the copyeditor was doing with the title. Let's leave it with all the French accents. But then the copyeditor may well want to italicize it, claiming

---

25. *Your Name Here* production files.

26. "The Green Dress" was eventually cut from *Your Name Here*, but is included in *Uncollected Poems* in *John Ashbery: Collected Poems, 1991–2000*, 756–57.

it to be in a foreign language. Will that be Okay, or O.K., or OK with you, or do I have your authority to insist that they leave it in good old American Roman type?"

In his annotated replies directly on Sifton's letter, Ashbery responded in the margin "<u>yes, you do</u>."[27]

I was not interested in enforcing "consistency" on Ashbery. Because my relationship with him was not that of an editor—and so, I was unable to have this type of detailed exchange with him—I sometimes felt uncomfortable making even the smallest and most obvious corrections to these manuscripts. In his poetry, Ashbery had a habit of using both British and American spellings of words, choosing alternate spellings over dominant ones, creating compounds that would ordinarily be hyphenated or separated and making two words out of what would normally be one (e.g., he sometimes preferred "any more" to "anymore," even when the word acts as an adverb), among other signature patterns that lend his language a living, off-kilter quality, in which multiple registers can coexist. Ashbery acknowledged these moments in his work:

> One feature of my poetry, if I think about it—which I don't do very often—is that I frequently write what sounds like a perfectly straightforward statement in which one word is slightly wrong or unexpected, or the tense of a verb is changed from what it should be. These bumps, as I think of them, are an important aspect of my poetry. I've noticed with French translators that their first aim is to smooth them all out so that they actually sound like French poetry, and I've argued with trans-

---

27. *Your Name Here* production files.

lators over this. They invariably say, "But you can't say that in French."
And I say, "But you can't say it in English either."[28]

My challenge, in places, became that of distinguishing these "bumps" from genuine errors. Since all of these works, had they been published, would have gone through further, if minimal, line editing (even, typically, into the galley stage), I made obvious corrections that, if left untouched, would impede the reader's ability to fully experience the text. Unless significant guesswork was required on my part, I do not note these types of changes (usually minor clarifications in punctuation and corrections of spelling and typewriter errors). The five appendices record more significant editorial decisions, and they hold space for the fact that Ashbery's intentions for these manuscripts are unknown. Each appendix includes a narrative introduction, including provenance of the manuscript and details of the editorial process, followed by notes organized according to each poem's unique structure. I hope that these appendices will be useful to those interested in examining editorial decisions and textual variants. I've also included information regarding Ashbery's many references, where appropriate, but this is by no means exhaustive, as I didn't wish to oversaturate the text of a poet skeptical of academic intrusion with interpretive notes or factoids. As Ashbery himself warns in the seventh poem of *The Art of Finger Dexterity*, "Changing Fingers on the Same Key":

> Orderly soul,
> looking for a way in telling
> us about dismangling—in a book?—

---

28. Ashbery and Rothenberg, "A Conversation on Music and Literature."

the way in is reversed now.
You bungle candor in issuing
an edition with notes—
what manner can they confine,
what new subjects elide
whose wan exegesis never tattled?[29]

The manuscripts and drafts in their original state, along with supplementary materials, will eventually be reunited with Ashbery's other papers at Harvard.

The poet Farnoosh Fathi, who served as a coeditor for this project in its foundational phases, set an early precedent for staying as true to the original manuscripts as possible. Fathi consulted closely with Ashbery during her important work collecting and editing *Joan Murray: Drafts, Fragments, and Poems*. Ashbery, always seeking out the work of underacknowledged poets, was a great admirer of Murray's sublime and vivid poetry. In his preface to the 2018 volume, Ashbery praises Fathi's work as an editor, writing, "It's as if the texts are given new space to breathe."[30]

Fathi's deep knowledge of Ashbery's work, combined with her expertise in preparing unconventional, unfinalized work for publication, had a significant influence on both the conceptual and editorial processes of this book. Fathi and I explored the basement archives of Ashbery and Kermani's Hudson home together and worked closely with Kermani to develop an editorial method that would fit within Ash-

---

29. *Parallel Movement of the Hands*, 53.

30. John Ashbery, preface to *Joan Murray: Drafts, Fragments, and Poems: The Complete Poetry*, ed. Farnoosh Fathi. New York Review Books, 2018, xvii.

bery's history of writing and publishing. Her early work envisioning the scope of the collection, studying and helping to select the manuscripts, proofing, and conducting research, was pivotal in shaping this book—and for this I am endlessly grateful.

For to be finished / is nothing.

The word "unfinished" and the idea of "unfinishedness" was something that both Fathi and I grappled with and reconceptualized during the early editing process. The five works presented in this collection exhibit their state of finish in completely different ways. The word "unfinished" seems more accurate and open than, say, "incomplete," which suggests something missing. For example, if we did not know from supplementary archival material that Ashbery was planning to complete poems for all fifty variations in Czerny's *The Art of Finger Dexterity*, we might experience this as a completed work. It is true that some of the poems do not appear to have reached the final stage of their project; the boundaries or edges of the text (usually around the end) seem open, a drop-off much like the serial cliffhangers Ashbery engages in *The Kane Richmond Project*. Other qualities of unfinishedness appear in the uncorrected state of some of the manuscripts, which may not have gone through the multiple-drafting processes of Ashbery's published works.

This is not the first time John Ashbery's unfinished works have been retrieved. His collaborative novel, *A Nest of Ninnies* (1969), cowritten with poet James Schuyler—a manuscript that both poets began in 1952, before Ashbery's long period of living in Paris—lay unfinished for over a decade before an editor suggested they pick the project back up and publish it.[31] And, in January 2009, Ashbery gave filmmaker Guy Maddin a photocopy of an "abandoned" eighty-nine-page play for possible use in his 2016 project *Seances,* in which "lost films" were re-created.[32] Ashbery promised to hand over this highly collaged play on the very same day he sent Maddin the text of "How to Take a Bath," a humorous prose poem written for Maddin's 2015 film *The Forbidden Room.*

In his email to Maddin, Ashbery describes this unfinished text:

> A hulk of a play I wrote during the early 70s, totally crazy, collaged from many sources including plays by Hermann Bahr and [Hermann] Sudermann, as well as encyclopedias and comic strips (one is Mary Worth for 1/16/74, the only way I've been able to date it.) . . . I thought I might copy it and send it to you, and you might be able to cherry-pick stuff to go with the lost movies, some of which sound like the materials I collaged. (Some of the parts that sound collaged are actually by me, though I may never remember which are which.) . . . The provisional title (still very provisional) is "The Inn of the Guardian Angel," the title of a book by the Comtesse de Ségur, 19th century children's book author (e.g., *Les Malheurs de Sophie*).[33]

Ashbery recalls that he couldn't quite figure out how to proceed with the play and "gradually stopped writing it," though he remembers giv-

---

31. John Ashbery, "The Making of John Ashbery and James Schuyler's *A Nest of Ninnies,*" *Context,* Dalkey Archive Press, 22 (2008), www.dalkeyarchive.com/the-making-of-john-ashbery-and-james-schuylers-a-nest-of-ninnies/.

32. I first came to know of this play while transcribing Ashbery's answers to an interview with the poet and scholar David Spittle. John Ashbery and David Spittle, "An Interview with John Ashbery," *The Midnight Mollusc* (blog), Sep.15, 2016, themidnightmollusc.blogspot.com/2016/09/an-interview-with-john-ashbery.html.

33. John Ashbery, correspondence with Guy Maddin, Dec. 2009. Courtesy of Guy Maddin.

ing a reading from it at the Drawing Center in New York City in the late 1970s with fiction writer Donald Barthelme.[34] As was typical of Ashbery's generous, collaborative spirit, he gave Maddin permission "to fool around with this text or any of mine that you might use— cut it, drown it out, mistreat it in any ways that seem appropriate."[35] Thanks to Maddin, I've had the privilege of seeing the typescript of "The Inn of the Guardian Angel"; it is an incredible play, with highly developed characters and witty dialogue, full of Ashbery's wide-ranging references. But what most struck me is the dedicated manner in which Ashbery kept track of his collaged sources. These include lines from Chekhov; *New York Daily News* clippings from 1972; *New York Times* obituaries; a play, *The Dawn*, by symbolist poet Émile Verhaeren; the children's play *Christmas With the Mulligans, Three Hundred Things a Bright Boy Can Do;*[36] and Gustav Wied's comedic four-act play $2 \times 2 = 5$, among many others. Ashbery noted the title of the work, and sometimes author, page number, even edition, in the margin or body of the play typescript itself, to mark such moments of intertextuality. This is a shared trait with several of the manuscripts in this book. Here, I have omitted these annotative referential notes from the text and included them in the appendices. However, as I re-searched each one, I began to wonder, "Who were they for?" Were they for Ashbery, whose linguistic malleability and tonal virtuosity perhaps made it difficult for him to remember what language was his

---

34. Ibid.

35. Ibid.

36. Excerpts from this 1911 hobby book for young boys also appear throughout Ashbery's long poem "The Skaters," which ends his collection *Rivers and Mountains* (1966). Ashbery noted this source on the first original typescript page of "The Skaters."

and what was not, or were they for an imagined other: someone like me, who might look in on these works in the future? Regardless of their intended reader, these internal citations are a marker of extreme care, an indication that Ashbery considered these poems to possess a future.

Having access to the unfinished works of our favorite artists is incredibly exciting, almost voyeuristic, like looking through a plexiglass peephole onto the bones of a construction site. There is something intimate about working with original manuscripts: in seeing the corrections, the thought process, the additions and subtractions. Ashbery shared this fascination with unfinished work. In an interview with Mark Ford, he describes his delight looking at Jacques-Louis David's unfinished painting, *Le Serment du Jeu de paume*. Ashbery originally wanted this image on the cover of his book *The Tennis Court Oath*, but the publisher ultimately rejected the idea. He commented, "I found some wonderful David drawings for that painting; before he did paintings of clothed people he drew them naked, and then after he'd do them with clothes—so there are drawings of naked men waving their hats in the air."[37] Later, Ashbery adds that these men-in-progress "leaping joyfully in the air ... create[d] a rather bizarre effect."[38] Here, Ashbery notices and admires the hidden movement within figures suspended not only in motion but in the animated dishabille of an artist's process. As in an Ashbery poem, which mimics the energy of mental life, a kinetic unresolvedness can be far more fascinating than a static finish.

---

37. John Ashbery and Mark Ford, *John Ashbery in Conversation with Mark Ford*. Between the Lines, 2003, 47. What Ashbery describes here is closer to the nude sketches on the unfinished painting itself, in which only the faces of the men are painted. The male figures are clothed in David's early sketches of the painting.

38. John Ashbery, transcript of handwritten annotations to *The Tennis Court Oath* (1962) for PEN America/First Editions, Second Thoughts, Mar.–Apr. 2014. Transcribed by ES.

This mid-air feeling, as it relates to process, echoes in Ashbery's use of the word "tentative" to describe the paintings of Jane Freilicher. The word becomes a kind of refrain throughout Ashbery's 1986 catalog essay on the New York School painter, revealing his propensity toward the inconclusive and provisional in art: "They struck me at first as tentative, a quality I have since come to admire and consider one of her strengths, having concluded that most good things are tentative, or should be if they aren't."[39] Later in this piece, Ashbery elaborates on this quality, adding,

> her realism is far from the "magic" kind that tries to conceal the effort behind its making and pretends to have sprung full-blown onto the canvas. . . . That is what I meant by "tentative." Nothing is ever taken for granted; the paintings do not look as if they took themselves for granted, and they remind us that we shouldn't take ourselves for granted either. Each is like a separate and valuable life coming into being. . . . The artists of the world can be divided into two groups: those who organize and premeditate, and those who accept the tentative, the whatever-happens-along. And though neither method is inherently superior, and one must always proceed by cases, I probably prefer more works of art that fall in the latter category.[40]

I remember the enthusiastic shiver that went through New York City around the 2016 opening of an early show at The Met Breuer, *Unfinished: Thoughts Left Visible*—an exhibit of artworks from the Renaissance to the twenty-first century, which showed unfinished works by

---

39. John Ashbery, "Jane Freilicher," *Reported Sightings: Art Chronicles 1957–1987*, ed. David Bergman. Harvard University Press, 1991, 240.

40. Ibid., 242–44.

well-known artists alongside "finished" artworks challenging the concept of finiteness in both content and form. In the catalog copy, the latter category was defined as "those that partake of a *non finito*—intentionally unfinished—aesthetic that embraces the unresolved and open-ended."[41] Ashbery may have told me about this exhibit, since he was always sending me off to see and experience things—the 2014 Balthus exhibit at the Metropolitan Museum, Jacques Rivette's dazzling film *Celine and Julie Go Boating* at Film Forum (to name a couple)—so that I might report back my impressions. It strikes me that the poems and projects in this collection inhabit *both* states presented in that exhibition: Because we know they are unfinished, we are invited to look into Ashbery's process and inhabit the pleasant open-endedness of these works—and, because they are poems by Ashbery, we can surmise that this freedom would have been (and perhaps already always was) ours.

I am keenly aware that posthumous publications of unfinished works are a complicated subject in literature. There is always the accompanying fear that the work was never meant to be published, was laid aside for a reason—that it is for the eyes of archivists and scholars only. I understand this position and did not take lightly the decision to publish these five poems—a choice that was not mine to make alone. In the absence of any explicit instructions from Ashbery regarding these poems, and after consulting with many friends of the estate, I arrived at the conclusion that these projects—at once artifacts of a career and exciting, ekphrastic works—deserved to be seen by both seasoned Ashberians and new readers of his poetry.

---

41. "Exhibition Overview, *Unfinished: Thoughts Left Visible*," Exhibitions, The Met Breuer, 2016, www.metmuseum.org/exhibitions/listings/2016/unfinished.

The Later Work

Despite Ashbery's reticence to discuss the meaning of his poetry, he has lent rich guiding imagery to his compositional methods. In a 1984 profile, he said: "I don't look on poems as closed works. I feel they're probably going on all the time in my head and I occasionally snip off a length."[42] Almost a decade earlier, he conjured something similar for Richard Kostelanetz:

> I have a feeling that in my mind is an underground stream, if you will, that I can have access to when I want it. I want the poetry to come out as freshly and unplanned as possible, but I don't want it to be stream of consciousness. I'm bored by the automatic writing of orthodox surrealism. There is more to one's mind than the unconscious. I have arranged things so that, as the stream is coming out, I make a number of rapid editorial changes.[43]

Ashbery offers variations on these linked metaphors of "tapping into" a continual source of language or consciousness; in an interview with Mark Ford, he uses the image of words "filter[ing] in over the transom" from another room.[44] These comments have been widely circulated, rehashed, and commented on, as they should be. They are vivid manifestations of the poet's mind—rejections of the "closed" text. If we

---

42. Bryan Appleyard, "The Major Genius of a Minor Art," *The Times* (London), *The Times Digital Archive*, Aug. 23, 1984, 8.

43. Richard Kostelanetz, *The Old Poetries and the New (Poets on Poetry)*. University of Michigan Press, 1981, 106.

44. Ashbery and Ford, *John Ashbery in Conversation with Mark Ford*, 67.

follow the reverberations of these comments into recent criticism and writing focused on Ashbery's late work and life, we can see how these images lend themselves to discussions of the shorter, discrete poems that have come to be associated with late Ashbery.[45]

In "American Snipper," his review of *Breezeway* (2015), the *New Yorker* poetry critic Dan Chaisson builds on Ashbery's 1984 statement to describe his recent poems: "But for years now Ashbery has been writing poems like those in *Breezeway*, short lyrics that begin anywhere and end with a shrug, formed from a bricolage of pop-cultural trivia and cliché. They aren't 'closed works,' as he has put it; they are lengths of consciousness that he will 'snip off' at random intervals, like licorice cut from a spool."[46] The "underground stream" appears (also in the pages of *The New Yorker*) in a 2005 profile by Larissa MacFarquhar:

> What [Ashbery] is trying to do . . . is jump-start a poem by lowering a bucket down into what feels like a kind of underground stream flowing

---

45. Excluding the many book reviews that appeared close on the heels of individual collections, criticism on the late-career work of Ashbery has been more difficult to come by than that which focuses on his early and mid-career, a dearth revealed and partially repaired by John Emil Vincent's essential critical study, *John Ashbery and You: His Later Books* (University of Georgia Press, 2007). A collection of artful portraits of Ashbery's later collections, from *April Galleons* to *Your Name Here*, this monograph underscores the craftsmanship, preoccupations, and discrete climates of these five highly individual collections—arguing that in Ashbery's late career, he shifts his focus from the unit of the poem to the "unit of the book." While reading *John Ashbery and You*, I realized that some of the poems in this collection might provide frameworks for new understandings of Ashbery's later poetry.

46. Dan Chiasson, "American Snipper: New Poems from John Ashbery," *The New Yorker*, May 25, 2015, www.newyorker.com/magazine/2015/06/01/american-snipper -books-chiasson.

through his mind—a stream of continuously flowing poetry, or perhaps poetic stuff would be a better way to put it. Whatever the bucket brings up will be his poem. . . . Since he is always dipping the bucket into the same stream his poems will resemble one another, but because the stream varies according to climatic conditions—what's on his mind, the weather, interruptions—they will also be different.[47]

In these paraphrased appearances of Ashbery's statements about his writing, the units of the "snip" and the "bucket" are (appropriately) categorized as individual poems—in Chiasson's review, "short lyrics." But in Ashbery's longer, united works, such as *Flow Chart* or *Girls on the Run*, which he wrote across many months, we might reimagine them as "entries." The "entry" is the unit of measure for many of the longer poems collected in this book. I have kept note of the dates of Ashbery's entries in a separate section at the back of the book in order to preserve a record of the frequency with which he revisited these works.

Though Ashbery's late poems have been characterized by many scholars, critics, and readers as short and discrete, the works presented herein, especially those we know to have been written in the early to mid-2000s—reveal an additional, "parallel" way, showing Ashbery's sustained mode of working on longer projects and serial poems alongside the often shorter poems associated with his later publications.

---

47. Larissa MacFarquhar, "Present Waking Life: Becoming John Ashbery," *The New Yorker*, Oct. 31, 2005, www.newyorker.com/magazine/2005/11/07/present-waking-life.

A Sadness Paradoxically Like Joy

In 2015, I helped Ashbery complete an annotation of *The Tennis Court Oath*, and it quickly became my favorite project we worked on together. A literary organization John wished to support had asked to auction an annotated first edition of his second collection. They would supply the book, and Ashbery would write in it. Over the course of two or three days, he dictated his memories of the poems, their origins, sources, and histories. After we'd gone through many drafts and corrections, Ashbery wrote his annotations by hand into the first edition. There were a few passages too long to fit on the page, and in these places, Ashbery would write "(see further notes in transcript)." We both noted with amusement that the Word document was more complete than the precious object it was meant to illuminate, and to which it was meant to add value. We joked about making a second annotated edition to keep for ourselves. This, unfortunately, never happened— but I remember feeling like I was stealing from the rich when I took the book to the copy center on Seventh Avenue and 23rd Street and gingerly pressed the book's binding onto the surface of a flatbed scanner to make hi-res scans of these handwritten annotations, which now reside in Ashbery's archive. These annotations to *The Tennis Court Oath* helped me to envision the format and tone of the five appendices that accompany these poems.

There were many times during this process when I wished Ashbery could repeat a similar illumination of the manuscripts collected here. It would have been wonderful to know when he first saw a Kane Richmond serial or what prompted him to write about the Parable of the Ten Virgins, or to have access to an illustrative memory about the line

"Eyebright torches the heart."[48] I struggled to reconcile my longing for additional information with my knowledge that ultimately it was unnecessary; these works stand on their own.

As a person, Ashbery was curious, kind, fiercely intelligent, quick-witted, sensitive, and hilarious; caring for him, his correspondence, his apartment, his poetry, and his archive in the small ways I could was the greatest privilege. Throughout this process, I tried to think of the work I was doing as an extension of my former role—a way of caring for his works so that others could encounter and appreciate them. One of the main aspects of my job with Ashbery was typing dictated correspondence and professional writing, an activity that at first seemed a vestige of a bygone era, but soon became one of my favorite parts of the position. Through typing what he spoke to me, I learned so much not only about Ashbery, his interests, his life and work, but also his voice and his many carefully tended friendships.

Taking dictation is a strange kind of channeling, in which another's language momentarily flows through you. This can also be a lot like writing poetry, as with Orpheus—the poet character in one of Ashbery's favorite films, Jean Cocteau's *Orphée* (1950)—who grasped for fragments of poetry transmitted over a car radio frequency from the underworld. During my research for this collection, it was bizarre and wonderful to encounter correspondence and even interview questions that felt oddly familiar, texts I would slowly realize that I'd typed myself. On August 29, 2017, the last time I saw John, I took the train up to Hudson from New York City, bringing with me a stash of bourbon-laced fudge brownies he liked from a local shop. That day,

---

48. *Parallel Movement of the Hands*, 21.

he dictated seven pages of correspondence to poets, acquaintances, fans, and friends. He passed away five days later. Transcribing these poems carried with it the closest feeling since his death of taking dictation. It felt like being with him again.

It was my habit when working with Ashbery, before the day's work began, to sneak into his office—located on the side of the apartment that faced the Hudson River (a nearly panoramic view that often brought to mind the canvases of Jane Freilicher, still-life paintings that so seamlessly collapsed the interior with the exterior)—and peek at Ashbery's typewriter to see what he had written the previous day. One morning, what I found there was this short prose poem, entitled "Homeless Heart":

> When I think of finishing the work, when I think of the finished work, a great sadness overtakes me, a sadness paradoxically like joy. The circumstances of doing put away, the being of it takes possession, like a tenant in a rented house. Where are you now, homeless heart? Caught in a hinge, or secreted behind drywall, like your nameless predecessors now that they have been given names? Best not to dwell on our situation, but to dwell in it is deeply refreshing. Like a sideboard covered with decanters and fruit. As a box kite is to a kite. The inside of stumbling. The way to breath. The caricature on the blackboard.[49]

When John emerged from his bedroom, I asked him about the poem, telling him how moved I was by it.

"I'm not sure about it," he responded. "You *really* like it?"

I urged him, as did many others, to include the poem in his next

---

49. John Ashbery, "Homeless Heart," *Quick Question*. Ecco/HarperCollins, 2012, 42.

collection, *Quick Question*, which was already in the process of being assembled.

As I recall, his issue with the poem had to do with a perceived sentimentality in both the title and the text itself. This hint of something approaching the sentimental was initially what endeared me to the poem. But after many rereadings, my admiration has been deepened and complicated by its exquisite negotiations of paradox and difference within language—the way it expresses a feeling I believe many poets and artists experience upon finishing a work: a hybrid sensation of melancholy and happiness. This feeling comes from the transition between a work that is active, in-progress, animated, to one that is its own entity, essentially out of one's hands.[50] The spirit of the artist is then cast out, without dwelling until the next work is taken up. This eviction is echoed in the liminal spaces that make up the center of the poem, the hinge, the space behind the walls, which invoke an understanding of the artist as one who both haunts and is haunted. Reading the poem for the first time, I remember it produced the image of the heart of the artist vacating the enclosure of the work as it was finished, like the hermit crab outgrowing its shell.

A progression of enclosures, the box kite, the inside of stumbling, and the breath finally lead us to an externalized image we might asso-

---

50. In his book, *The Art of the Ordinary: The Everyday Domain of Art, Film, Philosophy, and Poetry* (Cornell University Press, 2018), poet and scholar Richard Deming writes insightfully on this poem in a chapter dedicated entirely to Ashbery, connecting it to the poet's reckoning with mortality: "Ashbery's work makes it clear that the being and the work someday part ways. This text is not simply a representation, a mirroring, but an enactment of relationships that flow outward and inward" (87).

ciate with a new beginning: a sketch on the blackboard, a space where the next creation can emerge, a trace of something to come.

I returned to "Homeless Heart" often while working on this book, not only as a kind of touchstone for thinking about Ashbery's attitudes toward both finished and unfinished work, but also because it provided language and imagery to guide me in my ability to dwell in both the *doing* and the *being* of these poems, to envision the possibility that others might read them as simultaneously in-progress and realized, together in a new home.

EMILY SKILLINGS

THE HISTORY OF
PHOTOGRAPHY

1993

Fig. 1. Photocopy of the first typescript
page of "The History of Photography."

The History of Photography

① I.

First takers, first makers.
The first sip of intelligence
~~expands~~ the diapered sky, already ~~erased~~ crackled
with the losses that events are.   [margin: Splats]

At the old treehouse ~~they are clogged~~ one is — Dust
with sleep in any case. ~~Grey~~ garlands that sway
like chains of mice. And up from under
the palaver there is golden food.   [margin note under palaver]

So ~~may~~ it be clean at least.
The first person to be photographed was a man
having his boots cleaned. There were others
in the same street, but they moved and ~~so~~ became
invisible. How calm I am!

                                        too
Baron de Meyer saw the horse and it moved on.
Nor was the lesson of satin lost on him.
It all came to seem a big joke, his cake.
Besides, who would care, a little later? later on?

Not the house dog. The twig of coal?
Not the letterhead, though it is preserved, shining
where tulle cannot undress the board
~~body~~ under the table. It is all a—how do you say?   [margin: e.g.]
—A fancy.   [margin: 3/22]

How could I have had such a good idea?
But you know, the way they all say is a barrel.
Times two and too much. I have been coming and going
a fair share of my life, and some of me is up there,
photographed. Like a chair listening to a victrola record
I experience too little and know too much
for the good of others and their bathing suits.

Then too, as much escapes me as a tailor's dummy
in a photograph by Atget, taking in everything and nothing,
which caused the rain to fall one day.

Another day it was fine, we were "bent" on pleasure.
Sure enough, a skiff comes round a bend in the Thames,
a glory in progress. And we haven't even to see
these men, small as pickerel in the darting black,
for its hum to come to infest us too.

And buildings rise one behind the other.
~~TRAINIXIX~~ That is the festivity in this sense,
but it's all like lace paper doilies, alludes...
Meanwhile another man spoke to me
about a pocket watch. I have it here in my pocket
and can choose to let it go.

Fig. 2. Photocopy of the fourth typescript page of
"The History of Photography." Ashbery cited his quotations
of Matthew Arnold's poem *Sohrab and Rustum* (1853).

["Sokrat + Reistum",
Dyprent, p. 109]

"As some rich woman, on a winter's morn,
Eyes through her silken curtains the poor drudge
Who with numb blacken'd fingers makes her fire--
At cock-crow, on a starlit winter's morn,
When the frost ~~flourishes~~ flowers the whiten'd window panes--
And wonders how she lives, and what the thoughts
Of that poor drudge may be..." In just such another way,
from a far, anticipated world, I beg
the reader's indulgence, I... It has been formulaic   So far
(from the French formule and laic), just as setting out   ∧
on a journey to a fixed point, with no notion
of what comes in between, and without fortifying   ∧ 's
oneself with a cup of broth. What about boating?
I prefer the train; at least you know
it gets you there eventually (barring
some loathesome catastrophe); it has the ground
under its feet so to speak. In a boat you are never sure of arriving,
or making any progress; you could be moving backwards
into a dank nether world not of your imagining
or anyone's else. So let's travel by water, if
you please, the light glancing off the darting waves is reward
enough for any fatal inconveniences we might inherit
with a shrug, and so all is vapor, and threading   ∧ e
passages through some insufficiently imaged context. A clutter.

laïque

Then--stay.

~~XXXIX~~ Monotonously rings the little bell.
Eakins, skunked by depression, opted for cheese rinds,
a lorry driver's running balls--these are things
that cannot be painted, pole-vaulting figures, Muybridge's hopping woman,
because one ~~image~~ sheds another, cancels its own credibility
in a fever of slight adjustments, ends up a mass, twisted.
It's like corn popping. And yes... I bet I know, it's
higher, in the petrol-scented wine we all end up quaffing,
even getting to like. Look, Jack, I know you're my assistant,
let's end up telling each other impersonal trifles, scented
pec'cadillos, and that will have meant we collided
many a day, had attitudes and took off somewhere, before a recorded
voice summoned up to this studio, made us stand, one after the other.
I bet you think it's my arrears, but I swear I'm
not in this alone, that someone paged me... Anyway,
what's important is how we like each other, aye and without clothes
sometimes, swashbuckling, or sitting at a desk writing,
not imagining someone is watching. I'd cover you with kisses
like a wall with honeysuckle, if only I knew how to find out
the right place to be in at this time, as though it mattered
much in time, for you and your sister. All we ~~did~~was step out
a moment and came back in, and the earthquake
and the fire following on it destroyed everything we had ever come to know,
every chance for order. Oh, but who ~~he~~ eds these? Oh, but
I know you retain a sort of consciousness of them, a seething
as of breath.

vignette

did

And the old verger, "like some young cypress, tall, and dark, and straight,

THE HISTORY OF PHOTOGRAPHY

I

First takers, first makers.
The first sip of intelligence
splits the diapered sky, already crackled
with the losses that events are.

At the old treehouse one is clogged
with sleep in any case. Dust garlands that sway
like chains of mice. And up from under
the palaver there is golden food.

So let it be clean at least.
The first person to be photographed was a man
having his boots cleaned. There were others
in the same street, but they moved and became
invisible. *How calm I am!*

Baron de Meyer saw the horse and it too moved on.
Nor was the lesson of satin lost on him.
It all came to seem a big joke, his cake.
Besides, who would care, a little later, later on?

Not the house dog. The twig of coal?
Not the letterhead, though it is preserved, shining
where tulle cannot undress the board
leg under the table. It is all a—how do you say?
—A fancy.

How could I have had such a good idea?
But you know, the way they all say is a barrel.
Times two and too much. I have been coming and going
a fair share of my life, and some of me is up there,
photographed. Like a chair listening to a victrola record
I experience too little and know too much
for the good of others and their bathing suits.

Then too, as much escapes me as a tailor's dummy
in a photograph by Atget, taking in everything and nothing,
which caused the rain to fall one day.

Another day it was fine, we were "bent" on pleasure.
Sure enough, a skiff comes round a bend in the Thames,
a glory in progress. And we haven't even to see
these men, small as pickerel in the darting black,
for its hum to come to infest us too.

And buildings rise one behind the other.
That is the festivity in this sense,
but it's all like lace paper doilies, alludes . . .
Meanwhile another man spoke to me

about a pocket watch. I have it here in my pocket
and can choose to let it go.

And when all is said and one this one is let go.
Dominated by fools, he was desecrated for a time,
then came of age in autumn, just as the flocks
of purple storks were taking off for another climate.
He ranted and was let go.
Recanted and was let off.

The slow burn is thus the face's fixture,
what it needs, and has to tell. Everyone understands that
as a convention, born to pester yet never
released, never owned up to. O but I could
call you and you'd come over.
Never made a dime at this swamp
and some liken it to haze, as distance is draped
in the mind of the feeling man, who then gets his share
of surmise and stumbles off to bed,
a fool in time.

II

Francis Frith released the pyramids.
Nègre produced the ogival mysteries,
Mapplethorpe the dissenting penis (O
astigmatic, in whose lone eye

a chain of flattened stereoscopic eateries
atones for alternating dark and light bands
whose subtle pressures never made it into history:
a time of sad busyness climbing into sadness
for the view, always the same).

But while all I need is breathiness, lesser demons thumb
their noses at the moist parade even *that* notion insinuates:
only a door, to be discovered sooner or later.
Meanwhile what about the decoctions of nature,
you know, nature, that some were swigging already?

It was in fact the door to the great treasure house
noted for its treasures. And all I heard was one goblin say,
"Grace under pressure is the only reasonable account
it can give of itself. But whence comes
this pressure? You want breathiness, I'll give you breathiness,
but I still maintain a drop of evil
colors causes and effects with an ambition wholly beyond
ambition, and that the sorrow is buried there.
Tomorrow, though, we'll leaf through the others,
see what can be patched up, and what kind of sticking tape
devolves to this vastness and would-be vastness."

But it would have turned out differently anyway,
besides which it actually happened.
Two were in the rain. The life ballooned up through them,

light was as shoes to a frame of mind.
The wind didn't know what to make of any of it
and didn't realize it was invisible, which would have helped
if it stumbled into a garage, disturbing the ashes
on a mechanic's cigar. Then, what time, what tigers!
Any of us were giddy. And it was at this point,
always, that the light failed, like bunting
drooping against a building's dirty facade.
Make that two epitaphs.

Some came up to embrace (i.e., "kiss") you,
and absinthe was sipped, a wry duet rehearsed
as from a corner of the room a cat emerges,
slinks off, possibly to "play." More girls kissed us;
like a fire climbing in a chimney the song broke, then paused:
was this today ended, this event?
Or could we carry it with us, always, like a charm bracelet?
I'm afraid some of us need redemption more than others,
while you, my little man, require but a slice of recognition
cut from today's loaf: here, take it and be gone with you.

And the others—there are always more others—
construe it by fanning out over an immense field,
some so remote they seem but wicks,
while others resemble entirely the people they've become.
Look at me, I ask it only for my clothes,
the coat and hat I'm wearing: it must mean something,

and my plaid scarf, that must mean something too.
Only one forgets the orneriness in which we bathe
as in tedium, and this, all this, the background tends to bring out.

The foreground is something else again,
though:
Not enough commitments or evidence to cast it as a slow-moving,
lava-like meaning, with some grids sketched on it.
And it turns to dust when you touch it.
Still, there are people here, and frying sounds, and smells—
you don't get out of it that easily,
and just staying here, contemplating a watch or a resolve
isn't easy either, though it can refresh like bells
rolling in a sulfurous sky, luminous confections
that walk you home, prop you against the front steps, and tiptoe off.
Be thankful for this. I saved you.

"As some rich woman, on a winter's morn,
Eyes through her silken curtains the poor drudge
Who with numb blacken'd fingers makes her fire—
At cock-crow, on a starlit winter's morn,
When the frost flowers the whiten'd window panes—
And wonders how she lives, and what the thoughts
Of that poor drudge may be . . ." In just such another way,
from a far, anticipated world, I beg
the reader's indulgence, I . . . So far it has been formulaic
(from the French *formule* and *laique*), just as setting out
on a journey to a fixed point is, with no notion

of what comes in between, and without fortifying
oneself with a cup of broth. What about boating?
I prefer the train; at least you know
it gets you there eventually (barring
some loathsome catastrophe); it has the ground
under its feet so to speak. In a boat you are never sure of arriving,
or making any progress; you could be moving backwards
into a dank nether world not of your imagining
or anyone's else. So let's travel by water, if
you please, the light glancing off the darting waves is reward
enough for any fatal inconveniences we might inherit
with a shrug, and so all is vapor, and threading
passages through some insufficiently imaged context. A clutter.

Then—stay.

Monotonously rings the little bell.
Eakins, skunked by depression, opted for cheese rinds,
a lorry driver's running balls—these are things
that cannot be painted—pole-vaulting figures, Muybridge's hopping
    woman—
because one vignette sheds another, cancels its own credibility
in a fever of slight adjustments, ends up a mass, twisted.
It's like corn popping. And yes . . . I bet I know, it's
higher, in the petrol-scented wine we all end up quaffing,
even getting to like. Look, Jack, I know you're my assistant,
let's end up telling each other impersonal trifles, scented
peccadillos, and that will have meant we collided

many a day, had attitudes and took off somewhere, before a recorded
voice summoned up to this studio, made us stand, one after the
    other.
I bet you think it's my arrears, but I swear I'm
not in this alone, that someone paged me ... Anyway,
what's important is how we like each other, aye and without clothes
sometimes, swashbuckling, or sitting at a desk writing,
not imagining someone is watching. I'd cover you with kisses
like a wall with honeysuckle, if only I knew how to find out
the right place to be in at this time, as though it mattered
much in time, for you and your sister. All we did was step out
a moment and came back in, and the earthquake
and the fire following on it destroyed everything we had ever come
    to know,
every chance for order. Oh, but who needs these? Oh, but
I know you retain a sort of consciousness of them, a seething
as of breath.

And the old verger, *"like some young cypress, tall, and dark, and straight,*
Which in a queen's secluded garden throws
Its slight dark shadow on the moonlit turf," had our attention for a
    moment
till some audiophile blasted past us in the corridor.
It was that April 27th I think. The glittering ferryboat
detached itself from the pier and pushed slowly,
trustingly out into the water, and we ... we
were all ashore. It made a difference, that time.

III

Not to put too fine a point on it, you did
fit that grid rather too randomly over the maze
of life-sucking tubes that forms its constituency.
"I've lost my patina!" it seemed to shriek.
And how many tunes would that help?
Legions of fans would it take anyway
to unmottle their cautiously optimistic ergotizing
of "the black or dark purple sclerotium of the genus *Clavicept*
that occurs as a club-shaped body which replaces the seed
of various grasses (as rye)" into a "soft horny stub
about the size of chestnut occurring as a normal
growth in the tufts of hair on the back of the fetlock
in the horse"? Who knew it was coming apart like a billboard
of a driving woman being dismantled, panel by panel, and there is
    still something
we can all do to outlaw it? I think we just might,

think we just might . . .

but the eclogue needs your OK

and so it is not normal just to say
in the drugstore this is passable
this not and I'll have that other
one

any more than in a bakery one should point

and the whole neighborhood collapsing like a soufflé
of sea or sandstorm through which a father leads his sons
to my office now that so much great relief has been
overwhelmingly experienced—here the bass clarinetist
picks up his instrument, blows into it, twists
his little finger in his ear as the scrunch,
minute at first, soon unwieldy, empowers itself
into legions of the unwanted, singing:
"Ophélie you too were a disaster, as much
as Laertes or any Osric, but I can catch
you if you leap from that frame of flame that is
your oriel window, soothe gripes, and in a trice
be back at my stand, with none the wiser."

Just as each bottle in an assembly line passes under the spigot
that fills it, and passes on, so too is the end
of excessive noodling foreseen in the stellar almanac I hold
to my chest. Let there be no more division
of ecstasy, an' I say it who shouldn't,
never having experienced any, except face-down
in the noon hayfields, once. What I buy
I pass around; all are unbidden to this feast
of the every-day, so I can hear its
partial music just as a bird sings
out of reach, within the edge of a forest.

Let all others come if no one
believes it, and sample: surely the credulous
exist amid the skirts of the crowd, potential
buyers of snake-oil. So we let the last secret gasp
out of the folds of a bonnet, or shawl, and then what good is anybody's
to anything? Furthermore the door is soaked
with spring rain. Meanwhile, help me out of these—I'm soaked too.
Give me my scallop-shell of quiet
and I'll be moseying along. The hagiography of this moment
is supported by meager underpinnings. That other woman,
the one I knew, was she here too, or why
isn't she here? I meant to speak to her as she drove past
but her pink roadster was too quick, the crescent drive
spanning the harbor too seductive. I got lost
in my own sense of locomotion. She owes me,
therefore, but is unaware of it:
I shall be in her arrears till my dying day
while she frolics on the sand like a sea-urchin. The season
favors her, they all do; all is ornament laid over construction.
The moulting seals matter little to me,
the sky tigers even less, less than was vouchsafed her
and besides, her niece is in Tripoli.

Building it up in the same old mystic way in the name
of the goddess grammar is no doubt one important aspect
of the way in toward the truth: if possible one would
like to concentrate on lively things: bars, fires.

Horses drag some notion of why we were put on earth along
ploughed fields, like a harrow. And we can't say
this or that is true, only a hankering for further skin
registers on the bar-coding device. This is true.

On to further encounters deep among reeds then.
It's the unseen meeting that one values,
for time is less, and the musicians' contracts are unequivocal.
If only I could range over the earth with you, as you,
from beach to beach, the silver of your embarcadero
pulling away in the celestial light.
This is a dream of happiness.
It could be mentioned.

When one dunce happens
out of the bracken, his ass braying, two more
shall take his place on the scoreboard. For to be finished
is nothing. Only children and dinosaurs like endings,
and we shall be very happy once it all gets broken off.
The others, then—no, no, you missed the turnoff
into that driveway. The others must lead you now.

IV

Oh, the legions of seagoing fish!
Like sonnets marching in order, each with its placard
and assigned colored ribbon. You dazzle me.

I've been very circumspect these last hundred
years. My tailoring is correct,
I think.

Like a caged weasel the heart tears
at its own underpinnings. Then what ribbons fly!

Tears tuned awry, nobody to salt them,
undress them. When you came by I wasn't quite ready,
just needed a nap at first. Then you crush secrets
as carelessly as ripe, packed fruit. I mustn't be the one
who undoes this, your coming, bad behavior built in
to a situation which sticks
like steam plastered over a harbor.
And the Brooklyn Bridge was so—

You count only the net cost
of pearls, you're right, your business
is one of the biggest on the planet.
Come in for awhile, this hut
of dreams needs repairs, but its raw, vanilla-like essence
will do the trick, be that one variable for you
so many would like in their equation. And truant you
likes the discriminating serpent, its eyes matter
but they are forgotten. Dreams razed the old
curling architecture, bulldozed the land,
planted new crops there,
there where one or more come and are seen together.

And we be on the sand more than each other,
more than to each other. A last chance of sorts,
gayer than the other, more in a mood to celebrate
the mood. Planted on the leeward side.

V

Opening sky, wandering life, the movers.
The daisy born to shed its petals
between lovers' fingers: *un peu, beaucoup,*
passionnément, that's how it goes
until the river that is the railroad of time ends
as it should, thoughtfully. And by that pagan tree
that was planted yesterday, until your mother and the aunts came to
  visit.
We all sit on chairs, interrogating the milk-white floor—
but no, that's enough boners for today
(not the vulgar kind)—the sistrums are tinkling
way off in the panel whose edge only we see
when we're denied the other means of expression.
And then something grows, like guilt, or a fan
with Roman goddesses painted on it—they are
finding fault with someone you can't see. A disastrous freshet
takes command of the sky like a magenta dirigible
someone is "with." They and others
explore the tunnel exit. In a trice things have shifted—

now there is no more nutriment in the husks, no water in the canteen,
which gets automatically tossed in the sand. There are only reporters.

And if someone from some other life asks to see
someone in your household, make sure it isn't you.

Last year there were leather carpets here
and booths for waiting.
This year the still uneaten time is like a peach.
Beware, it says, of cavities that may still remain inside me
for I am not a church, but more like
the Trojan horse, that might scamper away
at any moment, yet lingers, a dot of icing on the horizon.

And surely those who were already meant to know
have sent in their entries, and only I, a kind of scroll
or tendril decorating a pillar, can produce moisture
in the right eyes. And if the chirping of crickets
were what was needed, we could play ball
in the endless stadium, and they'd chirp for us,
come heaven or high water. Or if the Labrador scented a skunk—but
    that's
epic, at least by comparison. We stay close
to the niche in the library, the oriel will be opening soon now.
Eyebright torches the heart. Winter was like this,
preventing furring, though at the edge of the glass
the decimal detail twitters, all is not well in this

bell-kingdom, sleds and runners ravage the tide.
Other: the hoof scores folly, makes a deliberate
impasto of sunny spokes of sense, the end not being
told. We gather in this house in this valley
to hear the prayer, chimes, times one.
And water gouges, gauges just the degree of impermanence
resonating, razor-like in cupboards and alleys.
The ghost outran us
but in the end he too perished, brought down
by the love that is almost always fatal.

The invention of technicolor redeems
folds that were medians, plains too narrow for settling on.

One sees the painted gate as though for the first time
sliding open on the boundary recesses and what
contingency behind, its tuning fork pitched
exactly right, the hay no longer suffers
and I'll bet you there are bleeders in there.
Elsewhere: famine, folly, the elders.
What caused us to think
the guest would never open the drawer in his bedside table,
withdraw stones that are a no-charm, pencils
that belonged to her, an eyeglass lens
and nothing that wasn't a secret, so that memory
came undone, floated on the tide like ribbons, pushed
softly out to sea? And the Jutland
kimono, also somehow implicated

by the month's day, the hour's point,
proposes a confused murmur, takes
the rest of the day off.

Only in a haze sometimes we see
portals that are visceral now, transplant us
to sleep and bed, insinuating a denouement
that is for later. The round habits of jockeys
bore these off, even unto the trees. Then the eighth
day arrives, surprisingly harmonious, a fragrant compendium
of the others, informed by earlier ambition.
These meet in a sigh, dash off, to the sky
later than was foretold.

Now the old man takes his leave.
Courtesy wrenched from confusion douses
the reproach of his having been here. We all imbibe
the new freshness like a straw, a stem
takes us from there to there, like heaven.
And sometimes we don't know what the difference was,
what other dalliance lay perfected
like a basking shark off the reef, and the surface stayed
still perfect, red-eyed and dripping.
Come no more for trifles you ask—
the liaison is purged, the clef—bent.
And the broad collar of the whigs (prigs?) gets
folded under, narrower each season, until only a line
invisible as the horizon's remains to be called on

to testify. Time enough in slightly later
winter for the strokes that curb your back, whispers
in the antechamber, the complex yet simple business
of extending living out to a stray ecstasy offshore:
withers wrung, stalls swept, a stray colt consoled, mud
drained, dried, blown off into the sun.

And whatever conceit we had nourished
then is as a bible now: no
parent or looking-glass: the sacred irony.

And when he was gone
some passed it along, thinking this is what it means to evolve
more or less, like fruit under an awning. And an old dog brought it
    back.
(An Egyptian dog, the only living being known to have been killed
    by a meteorite—
thanks, Robert E. Ripley) And said this is what I heard was it;
you can't tell from just looking at it,
though you can tell it's the saddest thing on this horizon.

And others teetered in the mess that winter
was that time, got stung in time's shell game, and dazed,
came out of victory, to kiss girls in the street
and heard their names echoing from a thousand windowblobs.

For just as the camera cannot lie,
those who would be gone are beautiful, taking

their shadows with them, unable to secure the life-raft
of a memory to the solid-looking hull.
Look, and be off then; there is something obscene
in the way it proposes itself, solid, even lichen-covered, dripping
as though time had just discovered it. More perfect ewes
among the dark yews. Candlelight just to think about it.
Birds dropping from the sky, all at once, hundreds of them;
lightning illuminating an old lightning rod; weary bumpkins; robust
damsels. And say, does
Nova Scotia play a part in any of this?
Nothing bumptious about that, is there?
Then, sturdier than a flower (O
my sinister goodbyes) let the companions go.

Yes, someone always wants out, but where
is the harm in that, since someone also wants in?
Someone even now is battling blizzards to a place he thinks
is the North Pole, but is in reality hundreds
of miles from there: an igloo
with an empty birdcage in it
(for love has fled; maybe, maybe though, it was always empty,
its little door ajar, its cuttlebone holder not unhinged, still
viable. No, love at last left us; no use
debating whether it exited, for it is gone.
Fomenting crises was its thing. And it is happy
and sad now, tears streaming down that smiling face
like rain streaking sunshine. *I know nothing*
of that, but someone left an envelope for you.

When the portholes go under,
when the city lists, we are not yet part of the fog, or frost,
though the candles all want us to be. But we are the companions—
how can we be something else?
I carry my candle because it
wants to be me, and wants to be seen, being me, and surely
I will set it carefully down some day, walk away,
deaf to its plaintive squeals, though they are barely audible anyway.
Mother and son rejoice at the distance the horse took,
he that stands patiently by, not seeing anything
remarkable in where he has been.
The coils of steam over the manure piles are like Venetian glass:
    mauve,
twisted, and orange. There's always someone to sidle up to
but for sure, only one you, plucked away now,
rent by the subway's screams, in some other place.

And the flowers we used to chant about have left too.
There is one beach in your eye, one hub
for all those spokes. In the beginning you were blond,
now you are stained with a certain majesty: there is nothing like
    doors
with light oozing under them. But if it's certitude
you're after, go pray to the radish, in time you'll know one thing or
    the other,
and if not, no one will be any the wiser, grab his crotch
and stare blankly at a board wall. In my dream I forgot
the dream I knew I was having, forgot to proceed, hovered

restlessly above a stream, unsure whether crystals
could be dislodged from that cliff, determined
to get my life in order, get past it, if I could find
out just what "it" was. And behold, three trancelike
sisters accosted me on the steep path: the first says, "Your breath
is showing"; the second, "Have you any money for the keeper,
the keeper down there, whose hoary seconds tick with a rage of time
like hailstones in your face, though you haven't any?"; while the third
   only smiled
and threw herself into the bottom of the canyon
where the thin stream trickled, and that was the end of our colloquy.
And these three are always with me, companions
of my companions in grief and destiny, and birthday parties
with marvelous green and gold shining hats to wear, and no room
for sorrow or anything resembling it, friends of my complexity.

You can sort of tell
which is the elders, by their glassy features
and celluloid reliquaries. Too, fish come to browse
at their feet. If eternity lasted all afternoon
the fish-boosters would still accommodate us, contented though
   browsing
and a child selling pears would wander past, pleated
by sun and rain, as in your libraries the decimal
system tells us to. We are not angels, neither
are we nincompoops, who can decipher the lyrics of an old
flivver, and make up our own music to supplant them.
All then is—is it ended? You, who looked to be—may be—

the docents of silver patterns, are ready for the innocuous
shields of meaning, can slather caulking over the screens
of the porch of our memory, and, when it comes time
to reverse that palindrome, may wonder how you ever
lugged that heavy planter across the terrace, past the homeboys
in revolutionary clothes, singing the chant of licorice
dreams and pineapple—but it's still the fish.
They're still here.

It's like trying to feed castor oil to an elephant,
dislodging the grain of prejudice from the bracts
of the Olympic range, and then remembering to bill
them for the maintenance. *They* don't consider it that,
and wonder why the deductible covers it
anyway. Lairs
of lovers always stumble on this
pleasant but essential issue; what's more, the result
is already known in unfurling scrolls that constitute, in large
measure, the future. When the animal returns, dumb,
to its brood, there's no way to explain why one held back
a percentage of its effort, making its family romance
seem non-binding, an affair of the environment or weather
on the shore, that pebbles look nice in.

First, the animated equestrian film:
it's true, all its feet are off the ground
simultaneously, its fetlocks
and withers waving triumphally in air, the end

of gravity, that insulating dominance.
There was no rider in that instance, but later
one is glimpsed in the background, then
in the foreground, a jockey of moonbeams, soon
to occupy center stage in the struggle for aesthetic significance
as it grows sluggish and weedy in certain tracts or vistas
closer to our trees.

It would be morbid to wish that unmade,
ungrateful in the extreme to promote random socialist realism
to the detriment of spiral nebulae. Yet, steeped in late capitalism,
half-drugged by the echoing of received behaviors, one can't
help consulting one's agenda, finding it empty of signifiers, the
otherwise signified having abandoned the trail, at which point
Project Demented Realism takes over, leaves false traces
to be followed by future generations of poetasters.
The earliest known film of someone slipping
on a banana peel is lost in the secreted mists of time,
while apples hang heavy on the shores of Lake Ontario,
waiting for that prime moment of sharpness in the air, the coming
of true reality which shall brook no gainsaying,
the old languid tale of laundry hanging,
waiting to be sprinkled and ironed, so that some sort of
maze of sense may be navigated, then folded
and put away like a deck chair.

Then what of the ostentatiously unmeritorious end of this day,
wherein hunched figures plot diagonals toward a vanishing point's

finer grain? Tower of the four green western towers,
long-hated awaiter, what is your plan?
It's March now, a time of no endings, of a gasp
of distances, of only further revelations.
We keep sidling, sand into a petal, before the long-lost
son shows up, before the film crews arrive, knowing there will be no
　　horizontal
tomorrow. My cat assures me it's all only time,
that what has been used up was used, twisted into an original
error, that in a house a few miles away
we shall assemble and see dark, not caring, the wind
always attentive to one's cheek, and once there we shall see better
but see nothing better. It'll be more like hearing,
or . . . or tasting. Any of those senses.

The holiday was a heap of cinders. But since nothing turning out
　　right
was the high sense of adventure that churned out stimuli
and no one asked questions anyway, it's also a cirrus riddle
that got glued to some near buildings and a patch of air before
　　settling down
to doze, unexplored. Readers will reach that point
someday and mark it with a strip of paper or a blade of grass.
Pedigrees will go unverified, assumptions unquizzed,
wells undrilled. Yes, and the fault will be ours,
somehow. We can't pin it on the horse
or a donkey, and doing so wouldn't solve

any number of problems of which this ain't one,
though it smacks of otherness. Funny thing
happened while I was on my way here: a crib bursting with violets
with a violet-eyed lamb inside it glided toward me.
And though I no longer tell people my dreams, so as not to bore
    them, I
think you'll agree this was worth consecrating with a moment's
    frown,
gesture of genteel indifference. Someone left the radio on.
We were spared the offer of a glass of iced tea, but had to admit how
    in retrospect
others' lives have surely inflected ours, like the icicle
the Snow Queen plunges into all our hearts.
And we get up and walk away, cured
of our nap, of her lullaby,
to the end of the road.

VI

Get out just the things you know—
on the road excellent sunflowers, the ubiquitous *carte de visite*,
demographics in which many a man's face is lost
on Pennsylvania coal-mining towns, coming clear at the end.
Wipe the slate clean, a name will be streaming there still.
The music box's insane tinkle invades the ice chest—stop it!
Or bring on the Chinese water torture. Where was I?

In Alphabet Land, where hundreds of pigeons coo.

Then he's going to put in that wonderful girl at the end
and the book will be finished, though not the sequel,
or a second or a third if the demand arises.
Is it OK to lie a little? Because otherwise I don't see
how we'll survive the big lies, when they happen along
like wolves beside a mill-race. Still, if you wanted
to magnify the wrong that was being done you could reduce
them to postage stamp size. Someone came by
and the question was forgotten until we were about to go to bed,
but by then appeared no more urgent than the stocking one peels off,
the braces one unhooks. By morning the crisis had evaporated,
or was well on its way to becoming a textbook case.
Flowers sparkled from the bookcase,
prawns were set before one,
and white wine.

Still, I fear all this is somehow "beside the point,"
if a point was what you wished to make. Don't quote, or your own
lack of enthusiasm will show through like a stain; somebody else's
    words
get noticed oftener, like phenomena in the sky that perhaps
were there always, or only since tonight.
No more burgers, only cole slaw and fried onion
rings. I'll have a slice. The tenderer shoots are greener
though in less good taste. And you thought dining was all about eating
and conversation. Try the cherries, they're
very good this year.

You'd better copy the inside better
lest it melt strictly she said, lest the
lakeside byres and constructions release their reflections underground.

Then there would be no telling the happy few how multitudinous
they'd become, how many roses in what cheeks, what cactuses
posing as cushions, what umbrellas snapped shut
as an inverted tear-drop floated upward and the sun came out,
a trifle grimly, so it seemed
then, and now, eighty years later
than the boy and the passing afternoon.
But why put a secret
in a letter to you, next day the newsboys are shouting it
and I walk with an archetypal embarrassment, dressed like Kierkegaard
in starched but mirth-provoking elegance.
That afternoon the drivers rehearsed their opera,
which was the first one devoted entirely to them, and that made
for an amethyst diaspora-moment in the fugue of trees
and would likely not be heard of again.
Rain pummeled the train. Sex invaded the kitchen
causing the soufflé to collapse, the milk to turn. Dust-mice
crept out of the broom-closet and flitted back. It was a well-worn
way to passing the time, and when we got there no one knew us.
The offices had closed, most of them. It was possible to buy thread
    and eggs
from a street vendor, and inherit two bits for the cinema
but the flamingo-legged clouds jerked the panorama past on strings.
Hair and a blunderbuss mounted the
metal embroidery steps to the trolley

while pumpkins rolled under the bridge warning us not to be too
    quiet
or the carabinieri would come before dawn and the tents
of summer camp implode, here or on some more vital planet.
Even commas shifted so as to look slightly different
though nothing one could pin down, and butch-femme couples
    operated
the garage-door remote-control device. A purple Niagara slid under
    the hedge.
The water-moccasin sang his coloratura aria of evil and pain
and eventual, violent catharsis. The anthill redoubled its efforts.
Bar patrons sprang off their stools to interrogate the night
outside. Television antennae waltzed like *petits rats*
into tortured gold darkness suffused by tempests and their attendant
pilgrims, and the gala musicale ended as the chandelier plunged
into the punchbowl, scattering ephemeral squiggles everywhere even
    unto
the outside world, which until now knew nothing of all this, but
    whose innocence
was ending with a bang, a big one.
                                        And three solemn sisters
in sunbonnets put their heads together, wondering where to cut the
    thread
and whether it was time yet.

All day, in every way, the old raspberry railroad cranked out
    mottoes, proposing
its own panaceas, all of which in some way involved exodus

or were unclear to someone of average intelligence.
Witches noted that the hour had come to pass, and children
looked forward to a day off from school, but the chemist frowned
at his own alembics, and martial law was installed in the villa district.
Nevertheless factory whistles hooted irreverently
at the end of the day—there was no muffling *them*.
But a still-born anthem in a kitchen-garden mooted the shame of all
    this
and was heard, if distractedly, its name and address taken down
in the massive hotel register dating back to the nineteenth century.
    The ikonostasis
shed its false-faces and crumbled into the pool of stanched desire.
As unlikely as chromed bats, wedded couples
took a few paces in air and returned, having discovered they could fly
but that no good would come of it until flypaper
and chimney swifts were abolished, and Uncle Bert returned
to his casino-bungalow by the Dniester so that pre-revolutionary
civilities could be revived, and cherry brandy administered
to the sick and wounded, the wanting, the ravaged, the infirm, those
with tics, and those whose modest eccentricities could pass unnoticed
in most crowds, but not in this one.
                Everywhere you looked
tousled recruits stammered eulogies to the four seasons, then burnt
their initials into the trunks of the birch forest with a magnifying glass.
It seemed a hallucinatory way of saying goodbye, or hello. Both
were pretty much the same by now. What had changed was the passage
connecting them—so many doubts aired, yet the air
came on always fresh and sweet, and fruits stood far-off and geometric,

as though no human hand had plucked them. Yet they were there
and ready for table consumption, whenever the dinner gong
should choose to resonate. Yet the froth of activity
before mealtimes crowded the pellucid element, frosting it slightly.
What would it be this time, was the implication? In any case, a
    surprise,
since they usually go over pretty well, even the unpleasant
ones, on account of leaving an exiguous space for human dignity
to adjust itself, verify its talons, its coiffure.

Easy learner, easy burner.
The first photographers
who got it right knew what they were doing.
Then a second generation came along, happy to play
in the ruts already carved, to flood them and conceal them under
    flowers.
Finally I think there was a generation of downright fakers
though no one is too sure about this. Then, just before our "now,"
things got really interesting, and information was communicated
to the eye and brain, which relished it, and proceeded to write
in great octavo notebooks, poems and things like that: excuses,
    elegies,
love-notes to the laundryman. When they finally broke into "now"
(having lost the combination), all was confusion and unfinished
    business:
Some got up to stare, or turned to hide, or faced the profusion
    squarely, difficult
as it was to do so without a precedent. Tattoo parlors and the loges

of theaters emptied out, a great running was in the streets
of a soon-to-be-seeing, but then that was all, and there was also
    more to come:
a diffident brightness on our side,
a long purple pyramid across the river, that asks and reshapes
its nutty question.
                That's how we got to be old-timers,
why we stay on here. The pictures are good. The air is fine.
The nectar and food are fine. The sisters are fine and resolute.

THE ART OF FINGER DEXTERITY

2007

[AFTER CARL CZERNY]

Fig. 3. Typescript page with Ashbery's handwritten
revisions of poem 19 from *The Art of Finger Dexterity*,
"Tense Positions with a 'Peaceful' Wrist."

19 Tense Positions with a "Peaceful" Wrist

If New England resembled Bulgaria, both would
look like this bookcase that stands so moderately,
like a birthday, like "things seen from right to left."

And in that case, possession (nine points of the)
would interject its other meaning. Is this, in fact, Brazil,
which all foreign countries resemble, even
the United States? But If not, let us hide our toes,
fall backward into stagnant ether that is what
rises to meet us at the end of all days, of all voyages
in and from the parlor. So, my little sea urchin, swimmer,   *translate*
sympathizer, We must convert what is meticulous *tense*
into rigorous outcomes that will ripple back
peaceful to foreign origins, not wishing to know the name
for what happened or why we connived at it,
only that all points are equidistant and xxxxxxxxx pleased,
swimmer, sympathizer the part of you that got on with it.
and part of summer, summer, Tyler Johnson

[6/18/07] NYC

Fig. 4. Typescript page with Ashbery's handwritten revisions
of poems 20 and 21 from *The Art of Finger Dexterity*,
"Double Octaves" and "Parallel Movement of the Hands [I]."

20   Double Octaves

Did you get a hat today?
~~IYXXXXXXXXXXXXXXXXXXXXXXXXX~~
You said it fled from my hand
thereby dirtying it with the band
(Difficulty there).

Let Disorder establish itself ~~is~~ here
and that would be something
more than we have or what we have got
except there's no way in.
(Sorghum! But that's not enough...)

21 Parallel Movement of the Hands

Don't put me on the desk.
I was afraid I was going to die very soon,
On a paper spree. ~~IXWXXXXXXXXXXXXXXXXXX~~ Any nice person will
die very shortly. It doesn't really fit.
A missing dog or donkey (registered)
does the American state police talk show
no favors, just as in the past you coaxed
belligerent sweetness from the ~~edge~~ and then   *hedge*
it was gone. Color? Why no color?
What did you expect from the microtonal
overlay of minutes? And then when it
did stand up, it was like nothing you ever imagined.

There was an unshapely tuft where the chimes rang
and forever after it was solid wall.
Nothing so became it as its tiresome
leave-taking. We were all pretty much
dispatched to our different sectors when the truth
happened, and bombed yet again.

What registers no vibration can't
expect to be named a consequence
or co-respondent if the peaceful enemy is really
coming back to engage the shares that were laid down
ages ago and are now ~~is~~ indistinguishable
from gaps in the truth. See here,
it seems to say, this is a consequence
(though inconsequential) and all of what was first
only by dreaming itself into position.

It's funny about dreams; they
happen pretty much everywhere. That's why
you can't ever be sure you're in one,
or out of it; why the rules of assembly
never apply to you in the present, only later
when the color of time being is finished anyway.

[Hudson]

6/28/57

21 Parallel Movement of the Hands

Saw him run ing,
a sunke n wraith.

Rather than ~~xxixxkx~~ figuring it all
out f~~xxxxxxxxxxxx~~ in one hour, pull the mud
out from und r him, whether that e xplains
the Treaty of Hubertus burg or this or that
spring wardrobe, it's ~~my~~ my placebo,
with all the trimmings, th*the* way we
and others like it, just so it belongs
to us and them. Granted a day of
catching up we could ~~all~~ work within
the barriers foreign trade imposes
on our ~~in some~~ purpose-built, big casino
gazebo, your and our place, gliding
across ~~over~~ the keys mindlessly ~~as~~ in a penance
a dream imposes--otherwise where are
they going to get backing for the ~~new~~ shift
in ways of thinking that lead invariably to your
correct ~~right~~ address, pulling your house and
delusions ~~decisions along~~ with it into the str am?

                   It's   than
      If that ~~is it~~ I ~~do~~ endorse it,
our ~~the~~ citizenry, ~~the~~ commonwealth, society,
all rowing frantically away
from today's mischief as from a wreck
real time in pr~~ogress~~, never to congratulate
anyone again on the ~~fine~~ light that emerges
to bathe us t~~hrough~~ *they* we bear no responsibility
for, ~~it it mxxxxxxp~~ or our felicity.
The wind blows where it wants ~~tox~~
the wind will carry it away.

6/29/09

[Hudson]

1. APPLICATION OF THE
FINGERS WITH QUIET HAND

A light rain, a walk in the proverbial park.
The unknown crowds around us, then dissipates
like a crowd losing interest.

The day is like a battle, i.e. orderly.
Someone comes from anotherplace
to observe the losses inflicted on nothing much.
When there is somebody who knows somebody
the pavilions of reason wait askance.

2. THE PASSING OF THE THUMB

Noon on the busy airplane
and besides this may never happen:
perspective, misunderstood

3. CLARITY IN VELOCITY

What sadness knows, knowledge knows only
in it passing, like a large bell
passing fidgeting others who only signal
to the past when it is gone
or waiting there forever.

What I did I did already.
There is no one to make plain
particular ivy and so on.

Grief is panoptic and segments every
past questioning until we come out and admit
to our day as it won us,
and make it more interesting than it possibly could have been.
I love you, school.
Trespass in shade.

4. LIGHT ARTICULATION

IN HALF-STACCATO

The one who came up to me and said
part of the American muslin movement
depends on what your shoulders told
the speckles of sunlight is off again:
The great brown and black ships
have drifted to the north
and the helmsman temporarily hides his face.

Loop my stuff together again shall I?
Soapsuds will always be cheerful for
they cannot escape their gurgling future,
any more than you or I could cancel
the dentist and what he means to accomplish
within our pastel and hybrid fears:
one of her favorites if and when he saw it.

5. EVENNESS IN DOUBLE RUNS

O happy something

6 . CLARITY IN BROKEN CHORDS

By the next day, Thursday,
bank examiners blew up the espaliered
orangery like at the charm school
massacre when milady partakes
of mildness, all smilax and curls,
and through the *tonnelle*'s damp falls
as though this were a hirsute day
on the river.

Still there are races
of twins on squatty
savannahs where birds opalize,
twit bald demeanor.

Did that ever happen?

7. CHANGING FINGERS

ON THE SAME KEY

By and large, the anthill.
Let us fiddle into being
whatever stopped
short or came up as
we were on the point of leaving, and said,
stay, just a little, can't you?

Orderly soul,
looking for a way in telling
us about dismangling—in a book?—
the way in is reversed now.
You bungle candor in issuing
an edition with notes—
what manner can they confine,
what new subjects elide
whose wan exegesis never tattled?

Fine with me, guv'nor.
I *love* it.

8. LIGHT ARTICULATION

OF THE LEFT HAND

He could understand the things at home.
—WALLACE STEVENS, "Things of August"

Scribbled on the expansive mist, the desire
of many dwindles to us
and our "activities," wholesome
or otherwise. Soon it becomes apparent
that neither they nor I have any prise

on the fabliau's demands of unity.
We are aching neither here nor there.
The tent caterpillars shrug off the tent, and proceed.

Was there a maxillary half-buried in the silt?
If so, what were we doing in earth-heaven?
Times came to be, trembled
on the tilt of a sword's point and slid off
into the grass. See, there was no warranty.
It's not like stuff you send away for
and it comes and you can't remember
why you ordered it. These, our time, were like grain,
necessary and inedible. In time the minute palace got chucked.

We were standing on the green, putting,
and our recollections came to resemble history:
serious, but not too serious,
redundant—and so on.

9. DELICACY IN SKIPS

AND STACCATOS

People,
      half-hurled,
you gonna know.
You gonna do.

You do something else.

Mais non, je t'adore.

10. EXERCISE FOR THIRDS

Would Siamese persons
now curly wrinkles blend
summon to an earthshower
the woken dresses?

Or is it day
falls upon us?

Flying, screaming
serpentine kisses half-hurled
out of milk-cloud . . .

No but I'd like to talk to you about it.

Did you get a hat today
or turn off the lamp first?

Worrier. You understand?
Sun ratchets up her power

of another,
fainter apology. Moral
marquetry's all my study now.
Leave hence! (Differently there.)

Brilliantly in this snow
the incredible sweetness of this hour
why institutional light overflows
the coast-guard precinct. Swimming
is all but forbidden. Say, why,

a permanent coming undone doesn't damage
the fringes or anything near
the center of all fun and living.

Goblins have their say, while 100 feet
away a tall painted dude resists amaze
to "pollute."

11. SKILL IN ALTERNATING FINGERS

We mustn't overdo

(listening pretty)

Interesting to ask so unevenly—the hoary corporate logo that
    defines us,
bargain let me go
I hope we see each other again,
abandon myself to the dumb of it. Like all musical expectancy
so much depends on what we have heard before. The basement
runaround,

        thunderstorm equipment—
ununderstand?
Interesting
to ask so unevenly—
passing before.

Redundant—and so on.
Gray carousel sprinkles into the soul
what microchefs deliver.

Did you know that street?

Whatever our time enjoyed was all right.
Good to take along. But the botched time, warts
and all, pitched us a curve out of the blue.

Here, though, we are seeming to be in control. The light dances,
people move along, the street is here, is ours, you pour some coffee,
soon it will be a slightly later time and that will be good for us. We
cannot see us emerging from the traffic light, only that we know where
we are onto. In that so much is born, is said, and it will all capitalize
on our nerves. Exit smiling. None of them was singular. You'll have
to leave that goat. Sometimes it falls where it wants to, prequel, some-
times it dwells in the dormers of suicidal understanding. That's how
we first figured a way out of it. But then we were magically back inside,
almost without having moved. That's what it wanted to do to us but
didn't dare at first. Then it was as if everything happened.

So it was that our druthers descended to us, at the back door to a story.
We were finished and knew it, but like as not we didn't know it and
were unfinished, a work of art. That and so much else. Calmly we note
that here. It is merry. Yet the tide comes in on precise steps and that
is to be how we know.

13. MAXIMUM VELOCITY

Clarity pursues us like
being ashamed on a bridge—no two
people feel the same
about it and the slime
underneath, anxious refrain
of a too terribly old tune, old time
music, something like that.

Like my arm,
giving up its shape like a forgetting
water, the piles will discourage any
apt forager or soldier
on his day off seeking a clue
that will give this all away
some day
or maybe not, not in
thrall to someone's resolution
for a something day not recommended
to us. I say, bring in the solution
whether a candle or mended stars
not too far off on our path
around the shore.

Please be this visitor who sees,
not the one who tended

a vitamin shop on the edges,
rolling or coming around.
If frazzle dimwits our intensity
so be it. Land ho. In your memo
faltering to one plain disaffection,
be not distemper, why that is the course
and what ravens on a mere
repetition of inconvenience,
something to be sidled by. That was
the point of our opposition
to achieve the same bend under rivers
of glare.

14. CHORD PASSAGES

The nutmeg house, truffle weather,
that season's wand—"gotta
be responsible," Robert said. Yeah right.
Ministers advocate aid. Percentage
subtracted from total equals chaos, more,
where reckoning is factored in like plaited willow,
unsung and a joy to itself. Mucus-slathered,
boy ghost in keyhole mirror fought off dogs of death
and lost. Still, a loophole

might open of its own volition
in his stressed night and other chants
taken up inform persecutors there was
no night like day, ever again
unless sunken afterthoughts, tire
irons forged against a bettered time,
period of grace for the branded ones.

Indications of sonatine continue to haunt the white
ogre careless of the Thuille-influenced backlit
diorama uncurling down to this day which is
his birthday. The home secretary, more happy than
the apes he had interviewed over all the years,
baldly outlined the cleavage

between this man's supposition and the other's
random nostalgia blowing up with the night
in wicked afterthought:
O the shame of being born to causal episodes'
agog drivel! And the more people came in for it,
the worse the clatter of self-congratulatory psalms.

We all attempted to live up to it.
Soon there was nothing left.

When I think about it the total simplicity
charms me the way a wreck would, or a wraith.
Obviously there's nothing wrong with standing to one side
while the boars brush past, or invoking a ton of nymphs
if you want to: that's show business, and horse trading
as well. Nor is it bad form to challenge the deity
over pale attributes emitted but never
knowingly received. While there's a dead-letter office
one should be gradual in assuming and allocating
blame, lest one's last donation loom smallest
in the rear-view mirror's tailpiece.

That said, I think there's some point in listening.
You may never get over exactly what it was you wanted to experience,
yet neither may those who wanted to offend you at all costs
when, emerging from the drum in which you had been hiding
since World War II, you were struck by the freshness of everything,
even the gnats clustered at the hem of a curtain
for some reason, not wanting to get out
along with everything else: placid, and confirmed, but not
going to stick around much longer, either,
as long as the climate was divided up by an infinite
number of propositions whose sum equalled that of the passengers
delayed by the strike and anxious to get home
early this night of chiseled dreams taking the helm
again, Laodicean, an ass between two bundles of hay.

Otherwise you can turn around,
go back, I mean. Sure, others
will see it as defeat. They'll even
be right. "You take it right home
with you, boy." It isn't necessary,
though, to have your mind read by them.
You're what's being decided on, and that
weakness is your peculiar strength,
provided it's carried through, to the end
and its abominable consequences, the jackals
laughing at the moon till they cry.

They grow up so fast.
Besides, they'll end up moving back in.
Nothing much can be done to sweeten
that state of affairs. Nor would you want to,
given the ambiguity that tails us.

18. CROSSING THE HANDS NATURALLY AND WITH A FINE TOUCH

The fat ride, once over,
dwindled to taxonomy. And what
of the reader, she asked. And it was good
to have done so. Now everybody
knew everybody else. It was like living outdoors,
forms emulating forms for all to see.
In a minute rain changed the perspective.
There was a crinkling of names, a bleating
from off shore as the dance of the fathers
came to unroll. The sons and sons-in-law
began to see a point in this change-over,
until now only a foretaste
of whatever wicked weather was to come.

God freed up rolling stock.
The procession divided itself
among canons and luster. Fragments
of pokiness floated on the summer wind
like cringing stallions. It was all the random
lovers needed to enlarge on fireweed and infatuation.

19. TENSE POSITIONS WITH

A "PEACEFUL" WRIST

If New England resembled Bulgaria, both would
look like this bookcase that stands so moderately,
like a birthday, "things seen from right to left."

And in that case, possession (nine points of the)
would inject its other meaning. Is this, in fact, Brazil,
which all foreign countries resemble, even
the United States? If not, let us hide our toes,
fall backward into stagnant ether that is what
rises at the end of all days, of all voyages
in and from the parlor. We must translate what is tense
into peaceful outcomes that will ripple back
to foreign origins, not wishing to know the name
for what happened or why we connived at it,
only that all points are equidistant and pleased,
and part of summer, the part of you that got on with it.

20. DOUBLE OCTAVES

Did you get a hat today?
You said it fled from my hand
thereby dirtying it with the band
(difficulty there).

Let disorder establish itself here
and that would be something
more than we have or what we have got
except there's no way in.
(Sorghum! But that's not enough . . .)

21. PARALLEL MOVEMENT

OF THE HANDS [1]

Don't put me on the desk.
I was afraid I was going to die very soon,
on a paper spree. Any nice person will
die very shortly. It doesn't really fit.
A missing dog or donkey (registered)
does the American state police talk show
no favors, just as in the past you coaxed
belligerent sweetness from the hedge and then
it was gone. Color? Why no color?
What did you expect from the microtonal
overlap of minutes? And then when it
did stand up, it was like nothing you ever imagined.

There was an unshapely tuft where the chimes rang
and forever after it was solid wall.
Nothing so became it as its tiresome
leave-taking. We were all pretty much
dispatched to our different sectors when the truth
happened, and bombed yet again.

What registers no vibration can't
expect to be named a consequence

or co-respondent if the peaceful enemy is really
coming back to engage the shares that were laid down
ages ago and are now indistinguishable
from gaps in the truth. See here,
it seems to say, this is a consequence
(though inconsequential) and all of what was first
only by dreaming itself into position.

It's funny about dreams; they
happen pretty much everywhere. That's why
you can't ever be sure you're in one,
or out of it; why the rules of assembly
never apply to you in the present, only later
when the color of time being is finished anyway.

21. PARALLEL MOVEMENT

OF THE HANDS [II]

Saw him running,
a sunken wraith.

Rather than figuring it all
out in one hour, pull the mud
out from under him, whether that explains
the Treaty of Hubertusburg or this or that
spring wardrobe, it's *my* placebo,
with all the trimmings, the way we
and others like it, just so it belongs
to us and them. Granted a day of
catching up we could work within
the barriers foreign trade imposes
on our purpose-built, big casino
gazebo, your and our place, gliding
across the keys mindlessly in a penance
a dream imposes—otherwise where are
they going to get backing for the shift
in ways of thinking that lead invariably to your
correct address, pulling your house and
delusions with it into the stream?

If it's that then I endorse it;
our citizenry, commonwealth, society,
all rowing frantically away
from today's mischief as from a wreck
in real time, never to congratulate
anyone again on the light that emerges
to bathe us that we bear no responsibility
for, or our felicity.
The wind blows where it wants.
The wind will carry it away.

Someone, an ode or
somewhere propped up the lost
target and men-
tioned it. Later they
got to see what is pro-
nounced this time. An
ogress? Huh. Last
one she scared did-
n't make it they made
two over. One was lost.

The polite
trill at the end
of a thunderstorm's
not a warning—it's
supposed to be that,
one thing or another.
If you're a guy you
can *see* that—the invisible
type of warning.

And why
throw caution to
the *winds*? Which

wind? Why are you
up so early? What
does it *mean* to have reflected
and been gone? So long.

Others will choose it's like
an explosion that just
passes on and you
were a chump. So be it
and let the serious part
now be all the en-
gagement, dappled
meeting and all persuasion,
O my truth. After all.

23. LIGHT TOUCH OF
THE LEFT HAND

You're telling me. Or imagine a plate of cookies
with nothing surrounding it. You, rushing toward
it before forgetting them. Others came in,
seeming to remember. Then I resumed your account
and found it fascinating. Mrs. Wackey baked them.

It might not matter specially to me,
especially seeing as how I was in your debt
in this regard. Please report to green fringe
concerning this mess and the stars
that seek to govern us
or putatively sentence us to gas chamber
generation gap we could ignore.

Fish might run,
O brother.

24. THE THUMB ON THE BLACK KEYS WITH THE HAND ABSOLUTELY QUIET

Instead of having to stand, you projected
on me your persistent language melody.
The waters of the lake were roiled,
came undone. If this is what

bending to others' expectations leads to
I shall have to try again, but lonesome.
For the waves that came along
were the same as those of many years ago,

as though time had dropped a stitch
which became the world we had always lived in:
cheerful, and dumb. I am all alone you said,
yet truly there are worse things to be:

unfriendly, or ungainly. As it is, you
sing out of all the holes in the tree:
The world is terra cotta, and this
rabid citizenry is now coarse and at peace,

like us in a persistent century down the block
when all kinds of ideas were beginning
to exist, and as quickly shriveling to naught.

After that came a break:
Of course there had been a misunderstanding.
It was probably better to mention it now,
when the light is golden, than wait

till its energy had been siphoned off.
So it was that we became partners, fated
never to meet this side of the maelstrom,
or the falls, yet glued in an impossible intimacy,

as though the plot of an opera had come undone
and some spear carriers gotten carried away,
mistaking the bell tower for Mount Olympus
and the flocks for Venetian pleasure boats.

If one could but see it clearly, all over again,
before closing down the exhibition permanently,
why our tickets would be good as new, refundable
as a corsair's booty, but twice as glamorous.

25. AGILITY AND CLARITY

Doing it *right now* is a still unscented
option I wouldn't feel with if I was you.
Nay, better an umbrella of meat samples than
last night's bestiary asleep here in the hard grass.

It makes me think: why chasten the pedestal
for the statue's shortcomings? If statue
is what it is. Ornery heap of drapes
is more like it, if you came.

We weren't supposed to identify one another
But these storms that blow up at the end
of each afternoon illustrate a different kind of tether:
the absent memory that links us to the moon.

26. MAXIMUM VELOCITY

IN ARPEGGIOS

Thereafter
foils drooped.
That's what I thought he said,
trespassing.

It won't be entirely winter.

SACRED AND PROFANE DANCES

(DATE UNKNOWN)

Fig. 6. Typescript page with Ashbery's handwritten revisions on his very first draft of "ATTAINDER."

ATTAINDER

When the master of the house returns home unexpectedly he he must be
greeted, served and lit to bed. God help the slow-witted servant girl
who has fallen asleep or forgotten to add oil to her lantern.
Conversely, the alert, energetic ones will be rewarded with the gift of
his gratitude. And this is as it should be, even when he comes
unexpectedly as he invariably does. And who can blame him? Who knows
the precise hour of one's arrival, anywhere? It would be unfair to
expect the master of the house to both know this and communicate it to
others. It is always difficult to voyage, and to arrive requires a
special strength given to few. There is so much effort involved in all
that, the moment of arrival that is like a somber overture, rustling
with questions that the seemingly more difficult voyage suppressed or
answered in a less than frank manner. Therefore it is good that the
master should be served; his efforts and his appetites demand it.

Maldoror considered these things, shifting his weight from hip to
hip, and then went over to the corner to question the view from his
window. This evil that I feel, that I taste, that makes the roads
slick, is there no end, no fruition to it? It comes from somewhere,
sufficient to find out where. For evil is almost the same as eveil, an
awakening, as when the master of the house arrives in a clatter and the
servants tear frantically through the house. What is it they are
looking for? Not the key, for they are inside, and the master
presumably has his own. Is it for the can of kerosene stowed in the
attic stairway? Yes, and something more, something to justify this
nameless panic, this horror; something as simple and smooth as the figs
and cheese on the plate, the frugal midnight collation, and as capable
of restoring the dream of order that has suddenly turned everything on
end and sent the groom and the stable boy scurrying frantically to the
cellar to draw a flagon of wine, the maids upstairs to make the beds,
four of them at a time gripping the corners of the sheet that bellies
in the air like a spinnaker. This is the rush, and it's not facile or
pleasant, but it does expand like a spring in the intoxication of our arrival.

ATTAINDER

When the master of the house returns home unexpectedly he must be greeted, served and lit to bed. God help the slow-witted servant girl who has fallen asleep or forgotten to add oil to her lantern. Conversely, the alert, energetic ones will be rewarded with the gift of his gratitude. This is as it should be, even when he comes unexpectedly as he invariably does. And who can blame him? Who knows the precise hour of one's arrival, anywhere? It would be unfair to expect the master of the house to both know this and communicate it to others. It is always difficult to voyage, and to arrive requires a special strength given to few. There is so much effort involved in all this, the moment of arrival which is like a somber overture, rustling with questions that the seemingly more difficult voyage suppressed or answered in a less than frank manner. Therefore it is good that the master should be served; his efforts and his appetites demand it.

Maldoror considered these things, shifting his weight from haunch to haunch, then went over to the corner to question the view from his terrace. This evil that I feel, that I taste, that makes the roads slick, is there no end, no fruition to it? It comes from somewhere, sufficient to find out where. For evil is almost the same as *éveil*, an awakening, as when the master arrives amid a clatter and the servants tear frantically through the house. What is it they are looking for? Not the key, for they are inside, and the master presumably has his own. Is it for the can of kerosene stowed in the attic stairway? Yes, and something more, something to justify this nameless panic, this horror; something as simple and smooth as the figs and cheese on the plate, the frugal midnight collation, and as capable of restoring the dream of order that has suddenly turned everything on end and sent the valet scurrying to the cellar to draw a flagon of wine, the maids upstairs to make the beds, four of them at a time gripping the corners of a sheet that bellies in the air like a spinnaker. This is the rush, and it's not facile or pleasant, but it does expand like a metal coil in the intoxication of arriving.

The soul, he thought, with its human faculties which put it in immediate touch with the universe, is a divine instrument, an aeolian harp which is not played upon by the winds of chance but by all the winds of despair that blow from the four quarters of human nature; and this music of the soul is a divine harmony which the creative imagination, alone of the human faculties, interprets in creative art.

What is it about the bridegroom?

While he was away, chaos under the guise of calm reigned in the house. The wise and the foolish virgins, or maids, tended to separate into two groups, with the former the most numerous by far. The social interaction that did take place was dictated largely by the nature of their work. The kitchen help, like the rest, was composed of members of both categories, and here as elsewhere much of the conversation consisted of grumbling on the part of the minority that actually did the work, and protests and excuses from the lazy ones. There were, of course, times when the differences between the two factions tended to get blurred, and something like normal social intercourse was the rule of the day. Such is the nature of work. We must of necessity set aside our social differences, or rather our social perceptions of our colleagues, in the interests of getting the job done. And this necessity results in an inferior kind of collegiality which an outsider might easily mistake for intimacy. In getting a meal ready, for instance, those who prepare the vegetables have to confer with each other about the details, i.e., is it necessary to cook the salsifies in a *blanc*, that is, an emulsion of flour and water which keeps them white, or would it be preferable to omit this step in the interests of getting the meal on the table, especially when there are a lot of other courses and time is short. (The salsifies would come out tasting the same without the *blanc*, though their appearance would of course be nicer if it were used.) At such moments the maids, both the lazy and the motivated ones, would naturally drift in conversation from the work at hand to more general observations, even to talk about personal matters. Trussing a fowl, for instance, would remind one of them how her mother was old and her fingers too stiff for such work, and of the lot of old people in general, how some age better than others, how some are a burden to their children though a burden one would never dream of trying to unload, etc.

Sometimes indeed the distinctions between the two groups would disappear momentarily or for longer periods. A kind of intimacy would suddenly spring up between two of the women, who would forget their differences under the spell of an anecdote someone might be telling, and this would lead to a conversational give-and-take very much like the chatter between friends, when we float from one topic to another and are drawn into all kinds of irrelevant asides and digressions, while our sudden perception of intimacy stimulates us to persevere in these bagatelles and experience them as a superior form of play, an unexpected gift that friendship brought with it. We get carried away by the intoxication of friendship, to the point even of forgetting about our friends while we are with them as we give ourselves to the joyous interplay of like spirits.

Thus, on certain days, the two coteries would have seemed to form a single homogeneous group, even to the schooled eye of a sociologist, and even the menservants, who considered the women as inferiors, would be drawn into the conversation and discover the physical attractiveness of some of them. On rare occasions a suffused sexuality burnished the air. The love that all the staff, including the lazy ones, felt for their master expanded to fill the house and penetrate the bodies of everyone. On such occasions it was common to refer to him as the bridegroom, for hadn't he absented himself to take a bride and bring her back to the house? Or would he be arriving with her? Perhaps he would arrive alone to begin organizing preparations for the wedding feast, and the bride and her retinue would travel separately, and the feast be held in the house.

However that might be, the master's arrival would be a moment of tremendous solemnity. Woe betide those too caught up in their own affairs to give him the reception that was fitting and which he expected. No excuses could or would be tolerated.

For though we always feel that we are an exception and that our lax behavior will be smiled on and tolerated by those who judge us, and even that there is something charming in our careless ignorance of the rules, deep down we know that such is not the case, that we are indeed responsible for all our acts and that our sins of omission are not picturesque gaps in the scenery but objects as solid and fatal as crimes or peccadillos we acknowledge having committed, though we still feel there are extenuating circumstances in these cases too.

And the true terror of the event slowly makes itself felt. The heavy iron knocker slams against the door in the middle of the night when most are asleep or passed out in a drunken stupor, with some of the maids and valets in bed together, and the echo shatters the midnight calm into thousands of fragments. What to do? It would have been better to think of this before, in good time; now there is very little that can be done beyond the usual rending of hair and gnashing of teeth, not a pretty sight when all is said and done, and guaranteed not to inspire the anticipated tears of sympathy, but instead a violent and almost irrational feeling of disgust. The weak at such times seem contemptible in their weakness, a sadistic criminal is more deserving of our sympathy than these cringing, bumbling figures throwing themselves around in the half-light, calling on God to save them, and yet—are they really so contemptible? Couldn't God begin by forgiving those who are merely "led astray" rather than those who stride confidently down the path toward evil, sneering and cursing at the legions of wishy-washy half-sinners they have left behind in their wake? Alas, it doesn't seem to work out this way. The hardened wrongdoers are if anything revered for their courage and impudence and end up as heroes, while the irresolute are punished ten times over, their appalling cries reminders of the evil of fickleness and dandyism.

SACRED AND PROFANE DANCES

What does it mean when the bridegroom arrives in the middle of the night? Was he tarrying at the wedding feast? And where is the bride? I don't know, one of the girls says, I thought she was here. Her place would be here, with us to wait on her. Yet she couldn't be here without one of us knowing. She is still with her parents, perhaps. The groom has forgotten something, perhaps the ring? He has returned here in a great hurry and is anxious to get the thing and return to the house of the bride's parents. No need then to turn the house upside down. One of us can light him to whatever room he needs to go to to get the thing. Other female attendants will be helping the bride to celebrate the wedding at her parents' house; they will help her to pass the time while he is absent, a short time in all likelihood; don't they live in the neighborhood. Yet even an absence of five minutes can seem like an eternity to one in her situation. That is why in addition to the attendants there will be musicians and jugglers and so on to help her forget the passing minutes. For us there is still time to catch a few more winks. You, Kristin or Laura or Lucile can unbar the door when he knocks and show him to his quarters.

And already the others are sinking into the pathetic attitudes of sleep where they were before they awakened and began to puzzle out their predicament. Two are wallowing on a mattress behind the great stove. Others are slumped on the kitchen chairs and one is even on the table. One of course, Lucile or Laura, is dozing in the porter's chair in the front hall, a mug of beer and a crust of bread within easy reach. The valets are snoring profoundly under the eaves in the attic; they, in any case are not on call; it is the girls who must answer the master's summons.

Why, though? Aren't they part of this whole household picture? Couldn't they see to it that there are reserves of oil in the house, so that the foolish virgins, when the master arrives, won't have to go out stumbling through the deserted town, trying frantically to find a shop that is open, pounding on metal shutters to no avail, crying and sobbing in the streets? They are, after all, not as "foolish" as the legend has it; they had trimmed their lamps, which is essential for their proper functioning. The oil business *was* unfortunate. But did it merit their being shut out of the house in the dead of night, their being told by the master that he doesn't know them? After all, he had seen them that very afternoon, when they were helping him get ready for the evening festivities. True, he was scarcely on intimate terms with them, and never addressed them by name. But from that to "not knowing them"? It seems more than a bit harsh, at least until further circumstances surrounding the incident are brought to light.

His return *was* unexpected. But aren't we all taught from earliest infancy to expect the unexpected? Even the "foolish" know that. Well, some learn their lessons well and some do not. Even such an elemental lesson as this can appear enigmatic and remote sometimes to someone studying with great attention. The words can suddenly turn to vapor or stones. They have a way of wriggling out of our grasp just when we thought to touch them. This can happen to the wise as well as to the foolish.

But there is a further extenuating circumstance for the silly girls. The bridegroom's itinerary was unclear from the start. Was he returning alone at midnight from the home of the bride's parents, with the intention of picking up something and going back, then returning with her and the rest of the wedding party? Or was he coming to collect the ten maidservants to go with him to the home of the bride's parents, after which all would return to celebrate the ceremony at the house of the bridegroom? This is possible; though they had prepared nothing special in the way of food that day, it might have been that the meal would be transported from the home of the bride's parents; it would be customary for them to provide the wedding reception. But no one had been specific about this, therefore the foolish ones, Deirdre and Agatha and the others, would have seen no reason to lay in an extra supply of oil; they might have thought they would merely be going out on the doorstep to light the master in, not traveling several blocks to the bride's house and then returning home and providing extra light for the banquet. They were then not really so silly but confused, confused about the timetable and the logistics of the feast, and about what their master, always disinclined to spell things out, might have been expecting from them. He, so imperious and in a way so selfish, who never bothered to pass the time of day with them and now claims never to have known them. Doesn't everyone have an unalienable right to be momentarily confused at times, or at least to be excused for it?

BE THAT AS IT MAY...

TEMPEST

"Poor Claire!"

"But she wanted him to leave her. That was the point. It has always been the point with Claire. Not to fail honestly would be to fail indeed. And failure is something she doesn't acknowledge, even to herself."

As usual Tempest's strands were many. In conversation she was like a fisherman with a number of lines which she was constantly checking, to see if some unlucky bullhead or catfish might have gone for the bait. But the little painted floats remained imperturbably placid on the current's mirroring surface. "Surely Nathan could have done something."

"The point, the rest of the point"—Elaine's tone grew a touch grim—she was fast beginning to weary of their topic as well as of Tempest's predictable analysis of it, though she was too good a friend to acknowledge it, "even to herself": "The point has always been for Nathan not to know. That way a brother can be flesh and blood—and Nathan has always been a bit too much of both—and still remain a—a statue. An equestrian statue. Of a lover, or Perseus, someone who's on his way to the rescue, and who never budges. And whose credentials therefore never need to be checked out."

Tempest turned toward the multipaned window and its implied view of water, just out of sight below the bluff. The Wildwoods had had their house built to the highest standards of conservative advanced taste in 1882.

There had always been a problem with damp, like a remnant of a summer cold. Today it was positively a presence, a commanding one, in the library, whose volumes of Opie Read and F. Hopkinson Smith had remained untouched for almost a century, and contributed to the temperature and smell. Something would have to be done about it, before the billowing grasscloth on the walls came down on them like a collapsed circus tent. Not today though.

"How odd to think of him with credentials—after all he's *only* her brother. Only and unimaginably other."

Elaine noted something like a "catch" in Claire's voice, and hurried onward. The afternoon was speeding along too, though it seemed endless.

21 VARIATIONS
ON MY ROOM

2002

Fig. 7. Photocopy of the fourth typescript page of
"21 Variations on My Room." Ashbery cited his
quotations of *Tom Swift and His Rocket Ship* (1954).

16   We reject these. Oh I am sure
     it was as serious then to be struggling
     as it is now. We were children,
     which made it easier, but harder as well
     because we didn't know anything. Now we have survided,
     you might say, but just look at the results.
     New factors have entered the equation
     but the surround is as messy as ever
     and even more limitless. The one city that accepts these
     excuses is strange to us. (It might surprise me.)   *It doesn't*
     The words had an unpleasant ring.) Hanging out with Baptists,
     drinking temperance beverages, is another kind
     of education, to which one is accustomed
     during the long nights of autumn.
     It comes as no surprise to learn that winter is on the way
     with headlands and diamond aigrettes, and that lightness.   *the*

                                                          9/3/02

17   Still hungry? Read on.
     Shopping where history and kindness meet
     two strangers clamp the gavel to the pleated wellhead.
     Nothing you nor I can say
     can undo what they said, but was it anything?
     A group of wilted children poured the tar
     from where it looked out on the film
     of ashes to the horizontal bars. Or
     it was arranged to look like some other unknown hour.
     A circumstance of such kidney as to bemuse purple assailants.
     They left the drum on. From the radiator to the city center
     it led to indecent bragging and imbrolios.
     Perhaps it's time to
     change the frequency of what is seen
     around us, leave the palace and go home.
     A chariot waits beside the door.
     The way in is blocked by the entrance, near it.

18   I don't know--spring came and went so fast this year,
     sex on the river--the chosen advice. And more.
     Once the foreplay is over the real mess can begin
     and one observes it. "I had no idea it was so complete,"
     Mrs. Swift continued, as they passed the dock area with its
     numerous boats
     and the playfields for tennis, baseball, and the other sports.
     The launching area is directly ahead.
     After that is the supervisors' area
     and you could go home now, except they are expected here
     and, wonderful to behold, are painted silver gray with a red rose
     and at the base were three red fins on which the *rocket*
     reckets seemed to be poised.
     "The one farther over is the dummy,"Tom explained.
     The flaming jet lifters lowered it onto a carpet of specially built,
     heat-resistant boiler-iron splash plate.
     A few moments later Sandy Swift made a perfect landing in a small jet plane.
     "I hope we get the rest of the day off, genius boy," Bud said shyly. 9/29/02 Tom Swift and His
                                                          Rocket ship,pp36-7

21 VARIATIONS ON MY ROOM

Ma chambre a la forme d'une cage.
—GUILLAUME APOLLINAIRE, "Hôtel"

1. The single best way to do it.

2. Resined and unresonated.
   Take back the adjectives.

3. Out of the pure, blue sky,
   to any functions at all,
   cheap and solid. And fun.

4. The single best way to do it:
   You don't have to wear wet pants ... I'm sure you do.
   Laws of enclosure a wonderful opportunity.
   You have an infected lip.

5. Home on derange is all.
   Homage to boys who won,
   not sparing the dull token
   of grief beyond all the wisdom.
   Who won then are no longer clear, ours

6. Making them weapons-like.
   A good grill for outdoor
   cooked meals on a closet shelf,
   peace and a sheaf of mental notes
   to put misery out of its misery.

7. We need to crawl
   from the gravel drive over
   to the garage. Newly ornate wheels,
   like creeper. Bands of brick, moulage,
   stammers masonry from
   where last let go. The pallor of Pallas
   overcomes evening do's and don'ts.

8. In my dream I was in Paris,
   upstairs in a large, rather shabby house.
   Someone downstairs had called for a cab,
   it had arrived, was blocking traffic. The driver
   seemed lost, and there were already passengers inside.
   Did I know where the Cinema Kriter was?
   Oh yes, I said confidently, in French. We
   climbed in next to the others, who were nice, disposed to receive us.

9. Every year at this time of day I get a feeling
   of a pain, like roses and dried figs.
   Nobody needs to know what is ailing me,
   which is sad, but telling them would be worse.
   I say, would you mind if I light up in bars?

There's no place left to smoke. I wonder about taxis.
I used to smoke in taxis, because it was forbidden in the subway.
That was before I gave up smoking, watching the flies
or files drift upward, wretched in gray dusk.

10. And if a child came over to play
it would be asked its name, then given a dose of brandy.
So as not to play any more. We risked it anyway,
out on the ice where it darkens
and seems to whisper
from down below. Watch out, it's the Snow Queen,
no one said. She likes playing
as long as she's not involved. That seemed to make sense,
but what was I to do, with no trains till next morning,
and a good sense of humor, someone said.

11. Next day the hills were parchment
good to look at from far away, which is
where we always are anyway. I dressed hurriedly,
consumed a hasty breakfast. Now it seemed there were pairs
of people thronging, telling me what to do.
As you know, if there's one thing I can't stand, it's that.
Turns out I don't stand it. People are treating me nicer
as though I'd stood up for myself, which is
something I'd never do. Father in his little house
took a bath. It was almost time for the news.
The trolley arrived in time for dinner.

12. Next day a disoriented child
    told you where to look for the cash under the sofa.
    We took a walk toward the cathedral.
    It missed us twice. I think. The pavement
    of white chocolate curves around
    the angle and is lost. Turns out it's lost.
    A patience or
    what happened is what the first place
    is considering: zebra crossing.
    And that doesn't include possible others that may have
    been reported. I'm ice in the house. And not the first,
    either. A tad mighty, I'm forever yours.
    His wings caress me nightly.

13. Turns out the bill was sent
    but to the wrong address. We have no credit rating
    any more. We must try to live without it
    and the unsuitable caresses of oldsters
    gone to the gym or the country. One
    wall features old billboards offering a trip to the seashore
    in forty-five minutes. With that, we
    can pick up and get lost. Far into the night the argument
    stitches its way. How long can we go on comprehending?
    There is more here than meets the eye. I was right
    about that. And in the name of solid fun,
    how much more decency can these elastics take?
    Plenty, unfortunately. So on my day off, I

took the long trek out of the city. My reward is solitude.
So get a life. It's been real. I mean really real.
Like you can't imagine it, so I must be going.
The city was leaving anyway,
closing its ranks behind him. Soon no one
would remember the boy in dross who used to come
and stare through the skateboards at the abandoned furniture
    warehouses.
And surely this was not a reproach, not to him for coming
with his charts and other paraphernalia, for no one,
not even his mother, could figure out what to ask him,
nor what outlandish reply he would come up with,
even if he answered, as indeed he never did.
So they got on well during the first semester.

14. The city and its pepperpot domes that day
    were a good time to be in, and out from
    the lattices a pleasant breeze was wafting,
    and in that breeze, mingled tones
    of melody like adjusted spices. Then it was all over.
    He felt well, who never said so. Oh. Oh. I don't know,
    it traveled under him, until he was going to be sick
    in the pit of his stomach, where ailments dwell.
    Nobody had to remind the boy
    to hang up his shoes that day, he was already in them,
    hobbling off to the cobblers to buy some new laces
    of the kind worn in the port city of his birth, but never
    seen this hour, of the flying kite, and the spitball
    hanging down, trying to unlatch the year.

15. They all knew him in that ancient, wondrous and miserable town
    as the local amateur historian and vendor
    of a kind of chili only the houris knew about.
    Then, as if turning his face away, he'd try
    to guess the answers to their riddles. If correct
    a kiss would reward him. If not, a turning away
    of a sheet of paper or promise to better himself
    in huge academic halls some kilometers away, but they
    didn't tell him this. There was no formal inquiry
    into his tousled penmanship, for all it led him
    unto the doctorate of his dreams and
    a cottage close to the bridge traffic where daily
    the seams are let out at evening. It was a pretty
    enough place though quiet. One has to endure
    certain systems, then profit by them later in the crust of events.

16. We reject these. Oh I am sure
    it was as serious then to be struggling
    as it is now. We were children,
    which made it easier, but harder as well
    because we didn't know anything. Now we have survived,
    you might say, but just look at the results.
    New factors have entered the equation
    but the surround is as messy as ever
    and even more limitless. The one city that accepts these
    excuses is strange to us. (It doesn't surprise me.
    The words had an unpleasant ring.) Hanging out with Baptists,
    drinking temperance beverages, is another kind

of education, to which one is accustomed
during the long nights of autumn.
It comes as no surprise to learn that winter is on the way
with headlands and diamond aigrettes, and the lightness.

17. Still hungry? Read on.
Shopping where history and kindness meet
two strangers clamp the gavel to the pleated wellhead.
Nothing you nor I can say
can undo what they said, but was it anything?
A group of wilted children poured the tar
from where it looked out on the film
of ashes to the horizontal bars. Or
it was arranged to look like some other unknown hour.
A circumstance of such kidney as to bemuse purple assailants.
They left the drum on. From the radiator to the city center
it led to indecent bragging and imbroglios.
Perhaps it's time to
change the frequency of what is seen
around us, leave the palace and go home.
A chariot waits beside the door.
The way in is blocked by the entrance, near it.

18. I don't know—spring came and went so fast this year,
sex on the river—the chosen advice. And more.
Once the foreplay is over the real mess can begin
and one observes it. "I had no idea it was so complete,"
Mrs. Swift continued, as they passed the dock area with its
numerous boats

and the playfields for tennis, baseball, and the other sports.
The launching area is directly ahead.
After that is the supervisors' area
and you could go home now, except they are expected here
and, wonderful to behold, are painted silver gray with a red rose
and at the base were three red fins on which the rocket
seemed to be poised.
"The one farther over is the dummy," Tom explained.
The flaming jet lifters lowered it onto a carpet of specially built,
heat-resistant boiler-iron splash plate.
A few moments later Sandy Swift made a perfect landing in a small
    jet plane.
"I hope we get the rest of the day off, genius boy," Bud said shyly.

THE KANE RICHMOND PROJECT

2002

Fig. 8. Original handwritten annotations and
corrections on a photocopy of the first
typescript page of *The Kane Richmond Project*.

Story ?

The Kane Richmond Project

(Spy Smasher) change title ?

A hundred major developments--
that's what I think about,
the sort of thing.

When the cause was opened
the singing stopped.

Man wanders along a ledge.
Vanished into the sea.
You both saw him.

Then the seething within is
wine to the dodged sense,
there is no whorl that knows us

or can think
about us
long enough.

The smouldering of brush
on the horizon
is a vivid sign,
one example of that.

Trout all told the truth.
The surface of the lake
was unified.
Then we all got together and pushed.
It was wonderful
for that one time.

Then old lovers fall apart.
We'll have plagues, good
times too. Don't mean
to think about that
or somewhere in there
the fat priest assented.

It was more than Mary could stand.

Dogs a-biting
in spring
is times for tulips again
and those other
forms in imagination.

We crept across a cornice
that was a choice point of entry

Fig. 9. Original handwritten annotations and corrections on a photocopy of the eleventh typescript page of *The Kane Richmond Project*.

Kane was lost in the Métro,
somewhere between Plaisance and Pernety.

Far from others he assuaged a certain need,
then felt better for it; the treetops and stars
danced and dwindled, from gateway to lounge.
Blandest of ghouls, the ~~lieutenant~~ sergeant
thought to turn the situation to his advantage yet again.
"Born in Milwaukee, I grew up in central Illinois
with little to show for it. My college education
left much to be desired. Life in Montmartre
was "twice as nice." Lord forgive me
for the occasional breach of bathroom etiquette.
I soldier on."

Memories of misbehavior
were ~~was~~ still fresh in their minds. They puzzled over a chart
thought to be of importance. ~~And then said nothing more.~~
Boys and girls came out to play,
~~and~~ the a little indifference goes a long way
toward coquetry of the sublime. This delighteness
under the summer sky is theirs, if they want it   Geet
really and truly. "The moon doth shine as bright as day,"
after all.

And then they die.
And then they keep on dying.
And then said nothing more.

5/21/02

                    Chapter Seven

The bloody creeps of war were not long in bringing an isolation to this spot.
Then I guess more visited it. It was not a sacred place, yet it was in the sense
that it was a place of pilgrimage. Rex and Rinty remembered it, Rinty perhaps
a little more clearly due to his dog's disposition. Then I guess the others caught
up with them, a few at a time. The war was almost over now. You could tell because
of the green light in the evening sky. Mme. Delaunay brought out the redingote
she'd knitted before the war and placed it sideways on a chair, it caught the sun's
declining rays. It was a wondrousness of zigzags interrupted by broken arcs toward
the bottom and what looked like shards of tufa settling haphazardly in the comforting
environment of the broken arcs. Long had she labored to sculpt the thing into something
like distinction, but it had always seemed drab to her despite the profusion of spring-
like color that drenched it and the surrounding walls of the room. She could see
down into the tiny square that was almost dark now, though up above the sky was light.
A few vagrants trespassed, for what purpose it was hard to make out. There was a urinoir
at the far edge from which men emerged quickly every so often, hastening their
steps as the sheaf of light from the arc lamp troubled them. The war was dark and
dense, but small now.
    Yet it culldn't be ignored, not completely. It was there like the beginning of a
migraine, the song of a siren leading to no good, but was beautiful in a kind of way
that had been formal before the war, like the stiff invitation cards called bristol
~~that~~ the postman would deliver. They always seemed to large for what they were used
for. That kind of patriotism had blent with the ensuing informality and become a
grave tempest, semi-formal as the invitations used to say. Marlise remembered one
evening being driven far out into the country to what turned out to be a truck farm,

Fig. 10. Typescript page with Ashbery's extensive handwritten revisions of "Sex on the River" from *The Kane Richmond Project*. Ashbery cited his quotations from *Danger on Vampire Trail* (1971) in the margin of the first draft.

Sex on the River

>   "The Mayor is urinating on the wrong side/of
>   the street! A dandelion sends off sparks:
>   beware your hair is locked!

~~I don't know~~ Spring came and went so fast this year.
~~The rookies one that year.~~ Not one
to beat about the bush, rootless,
roofless I go on. ~~In the dude.~~

I pick up the chosen advice
like broken watchworks--will it be time for me?
Or for some other--

Methought the King of Thule
sat by my side in the empty banquet hall,
a gilded goblet in his hand. "Here, try some of this.
It'll put lead in your pencil." "No thanks, King."
Like a madman he staggered to the balcony,
tossed the thing into the sea. ~~Which began to boil.~~

"~~How can we help?~~" ~~Joe~~ wanted to ~~know~~.
"By taking over the ~~XXXIX~~ entire assignment.
I've been asked to handle a high-priority case for the government."

VI 1,2

"~~But why the camping trip? How does that come into the picture?~~"
"Conflict of interest, I'm afraid.
He declined to represent me."

"~~Then where does the thing come out?~~"
"~~Below the river's ledge.~~" The old man spoke no more.
We were out of time,
had to be leaving
on a new desperate adventure
~~that was sure to bring relief to tired heads.~~
"If only we could believe it."

~~But you can son, if I can--~~
~~make it though the tired morning, that is.~~

Where shall we meet up afterward?

~~At Mr. Jenkins tired circle--the~~ turnaround.

Figs. 11 (facing) and 12 (over). Ashbery's first, handwritten draft of what later became the sections "An Unspecified Amount" and "*très modéré*" in *The Kane Richmond Project*.

An Unspecified Amount

Someone must have been telling lies about
John A. It happened this way: all day long he
would sit on the front porch, watching people and
cars go by. Except for his meals, which he took at
the kitchen table, he would remain on the porch from
dawn until it got quite dark, summer and winter,
except for periods of extreme cold. Even then he
could survey the street through a species of pan-
opticon he had rigged up, which he liked to
say was better than television, since it was free and
never required adjustment. He said this mostly to himself
since he rarely spoke to others, having little occasion
to do so. He was not one of those people who sit and wave
at cars and ~~pay~~ ~~greet~~ salute passersby with a cheery greeting.
The one exception to his code of silence was ~~floored~~ his
cleaning ~~woman~~ who came twice a week, and even
then his speech concerned mainly practical household
matters.

    One day a Fuller Brush man happened by, and,
undiscouraged by John's laconic replies to his attempts
at small talk, seated himself in the wicker chair
where John would sit to read the newspaper, and was
the only piece of porch furniture except for a glider
where he would recline and occasionally take a nap,
though this rarely happened since it ~~only~~ prevented him
from observing the ~~street~~ activity in the street.
Finding that his observations concerning the traffic and weather
~~and the~~ were not rebuffed, though scarcely encouraged,

Pegging
on
~~starting~~
his
briar
pipe

The man proceeded to expand on other topics such as the decline of the neighborhood. This irritated and frustrated ~~John~~ John, who had been expecting ~~into~~ a sales pitch for the brushes, and had already begun preparing a reply to the effect that he was amply provided with cleaning utensils and employed a ~~cleaning woman~~ person, part of ~~whose duties included~~ ~~to make certain~~ as ascertaining that nothing was lacking in that department. He ~~he~~ began casting about for other ways of ridding him of ~~the~~ ~~unwelcome past~~ this stranger, when the ~~latter~~ suddenly ~~though he was~~ startled him by drawing his attention to a large ~~package~~ package which the postman had evidently left on the ~~doormat~~ by the front door, whose mail slot ~~would have been~~ too narrow to accommodate 7.

"What do you suppose is in there?" the stranger asked, a bit ~~impudently~~ impertinently it seemed to John.

"Oh, it's probably some boots I ordered from L.L. Bean" John ~~answered~~ answered shiftily, aware as he did so that the package ~~obviously~~ contained nothing of the sort and that he had just unwittingly opened ~~up~~ ~~further~~ new avenues in a conversation that was fast becoming vexatious.

The salesman however let the matter rest there. Or was he considering the most effective way to continue to irk John even further?

fresh mackerel and frozen peas

Spy Smasher

A hundred major developments—
that's what I think about,
the sort of thing.

When the cause was opened
the singing stopped.

Man wanders along a ledge.
Vanished into the sea.
You both saw him.

Then the seething within is
wine to the dodged sense,
there is no whorl that knows us

or can think
about us
long enough.

The smouldering of brush
on the horizon
is a vivid sign,
one example of that.

Trout all told the truth.
The surface of the lake
was unified.
Then we all got together and pushed.
It was wonderful
for that one time.

Then old lovers fall apart.
We'll have plagues, good
times too. Don't mean
to think about that
or somewhere in there
the fat priest assented.

It was more than Mary could stand.

Dogs a-biting
in spring
is times for tulips again
and those other
forms in imagination.

We crept across a cornice
that was a choice point of entry
since it was logical to undertake
but oh my goodness—weight of the past,
strife coming up from

all that mortifying of tall ships
that pass obviously on their way to something.

Perils of Nyoka

The spy tooth—
it was here a minute ago.

The Devil Diamond

Years of fuss
have smoothed the way, paved
our highway to happiness in the home
and huge morsel of bone for Bonzo.

Night is again a practice
seeking help from the underdog
who wants to commit all these sins
and have done with clarity and grace.

A panel sits
in judgement on the oblique
charity of more years,
more than you'll know.
My experiment didn't sit
too well with the others,
ravished by sepia flames half outdoors.

A keg
of learning understands little
by little
how it means to understand.

Principally we are forced back
under the open throne
of sunlight and graves.
More nudity was forecast
than modesty did the trick
it being all over but the postscript
written in violet—
"This adjunct belongs to you,
mortifiably yours."

Old sweethearts belong
to who once owned them
flashing courage from
corner cobwebs
and don't mean to deceive or be deceived.
This happens once in a lifetime
after we are on the beach.

A logistical nightmare
written by a man named Longfellow.

The Lost City

Expectation draining
from someone (patent pending).
He put on his hat, longs to
be the shore, longs after the hill.
These are wide and spacious
and there are other, narrower places
that belong next to the man.

Spring was a little late that year.
She swept up the tulips,
preferred a destiny like an arc.
Meanwhile the kids kept on coming.

There was no stopping the cars,
they were brutal. He traveled
across the street. Now others
were aware of it. You couldn't just go
away. He sat down to think about it.
Others of her society friends
just ignored it. You could do that,
but not safely in a race of one day
over the night shoals. He didn't
know where his job was. They had
lost his name. He certainly wasn't
coming any more. The passage is clear now.
Others than he soaking up the attitude

of men die in a war. An old stocking
would serve to hide the truth
from her.

She turned her calves.
They were white, like the lost city.
It was all over for the time being.

Please, Earl, I just can't explain now.

Racing Blood

Of all the rotten excuses.
Forgetting to go out there.
Kane didn't tell them he might
go have a look round.
Nobody suspected his absence for hours
but even then they didn't think too much of it—
he was always off somewhere poking around
to see what he could discover, if anything.
It wasn't till past midnight one of them
looks up Oh crap he says. He might
have been found if it was easier to find out
stuff that the store sells. He got into a boat,
started bailing for dear life. "Dear" life?
Well, I guess so. Before morning had tinted the ridge
nobody was left. This debased feeling

crept over almost all of us,
little by little, like a rag of fog.

Most folks don't care to come out,
let the whatever come to them,
or not, depending on what they spend.
He had expenses that year,
what with turning around, accosting
yourself in a mirror in an old hat
lying by the door some cripple left open.
But just because the guy is on crutches
don't mean he ain't open to slander
the committee said. Maybe the dope don't
go out either, it's not easy to find
too many out. They'll come
out when they want to, blood racing,
a streak of blood in the eye
meaning you should turn away please
there's bound to be trouble
and then the sun looks out and sees nothing
out of the ordinary, the whole bill of goods
is forgotten and many wax disinterested.
'Tain't my time of life. Oh yeah,
sez who, you was here before when I
recognized you. But
that's one thing that's over now,
we can put away. A cow signed a letter
to the local paper when Arnie got wind of it.

He was fixin' in an uproar,
mudslide that passes through.
I tip my hat to no one.
Now get out please.
Only, he forgot to sign the check.

The whole operation came apart,
unraveling from the mountaintop.
Now one sees urban, the other's nuts
or strange, feeding the kitty, and the floe
seriously damaged crops of interest
for that period and that daydream.
Damned if we all weren't concerned and let go,
but tightly this time, remembering the last avalanche
when Dad was alive and springtime had come to the Rockies,
not daring to show its face. Damn, that
was some commotion. Still we are hectored,
he and I. Scratch me and I'll scratch you.
That's what it's coming to, to true blue.

"Dear" had life tinged on it? Not on my watch,
they don't. It was so casual of you, too.
Walking to me on the tops of the bunkers,
ones that you would like,
which I never saw.

And spoiling it.

Rudy is shanghaied aboard the Lady Letty
and falls for Moran, the captain's daughter.
Soon the kindly captain dies. Rudy's rich friends
have forgotten him, though he dreams of them.
Here, do it like this.
No, like this.

Complimentary or complementary
makes no difference. We're all long gone
in the long run. It is sufficient to be ignored
long after one's death. Meanwhile the tide keeps creeping
purposefully. A bat's wing against the night
sets all aglare. Rex and Rinty are a part
of the equation.

A wall of blistered sadness is all there is.
Coming down out of the forest, remember
the campsite, tales around the fire.
Now it's winter, and doesn't match up.

The pig-ore process proved too costly
to manufacturers in the long run.
Which is why they came out smiling.
A handshake sealed the deal
and it was off into the wilderness.
"It's—too divine!" she exclaimed.
The wilderness walled off.

Macaques and yellow parrots
congregated with the flamingos at their watering hole.
Rudy pines for the golf course. In a second he's awake!
And it all comes back to barter, for food,
for the natives' trinkets, barley and a place to stay.
"Yes—*too* divine," he thought sadly to himself.
Slowly, water covers the land.
It was an end anyway. No hiding place.

Now I had nine or ten pages of copy.
Down by the water cooler is vanilla only.
Goran stabs the horse fatally, and police in riot gear
converge on the scene. Supplies are running low
for the gang that sang "Heart of My Heart," but
on the horizon sister Anne can excitedly make out a figure
on horseback hastening toward the ball of the present.
We are saved, it seems, again,
but don't expect grace from the collision of truth and energy:
The fact is we are in retreat from invisible forces
that wake us smiling every day, hand you
a cup of coffee as you go out the screen door. Ah, but
"a world of hope and joy I see." That's the president's dream,
he applies the brakes gently.

Back at the White House the tin hygrometer solved nothing;
we were truly "out in the world." No, but cub scout packs come by
    to save you
in good time; the ogre's dream seems to dissipate but in reality he's

standing in the front hall, glove draped over wrist.
I thought we'd go for a ride today,
back to the little hills where childhood first churned,
lilacs whispered in the apiary, and all was as a done deal ten years ago.
These painted flats might refresh your memory.
Meanwhile a world's worth
of imagining might revive the tapestry, restore
the satin finish to the wheelhouse valve casings, let a little air in
around the corners of the portrait that has gazed there for so long,
a little sorrowful, it seems, though not inappropriately.

What Anne saw from the tower was only a mirage,
a whorl of dust like a genie let out of a bottle,
nothing to disturb our studiously poised question mark
let down from the heavens.   When I inquired later about the so-called
phenomena during the interval, no one said anything, though all
appeared expectant. The evening paper lands on the porch with a thud
but we aren't to be released, yet. It says so here.
"Society figure" (that would be Rudy) "missing: foul play feared."
What about *our* crimes and delusions? Haven't we walked the plank
    far enough?

"To observe is to grow lonely.
The dog taught you that. Try holding your breath a little longer each
    day.
But some of them always get away.
Pretend it's not you inhaling.

We may get out of a tight spot
or not, but one thing will be well:
that innocence bantered this far, almost to the doorstep.
Some fool around, but the 'happy few' (that's us),
will find our reward in listening.
A mixed bag, but so it is written."

The church gives you a dime, don't complain.
I have researched my position paper
to the fullest, and am ready to pronounce:
Big music in mid-disaster. That could be terrible
but just as well be nice, if someone likes it.
You've got to accept the door when it opens
on the mild mystery of the Falcon, in California
or some other place. He made quite a career out of being in them.
Rudy wouldn't have done that. There were so few places to accept
    him—
the tent, the studio. The end, when it came, left not a scrap of any
    of them.
And it's true you don't see the Falcon much in Pennsylvania
or Ohio, but he could just as easily get there if the distractions
of the plot called for it. Mrs. O'Leary's cow was an invention,
by the way, to distract people from the fact of the Chicago fire.
Nowadays animals don't go to bat for their masters that much,
though a few do. Rex and Rinty were never the same
after the burning stable incident, but did either of them let out a
    growl
or as much as a whimper? Kane was a loving master,

it's true, but there is a sphere of soul in those animals
no Pavlov could ever figure out. They eat dog food
are grateful to it, and get to run around each day.
Modern mammals shun salads or anything to do with pleasure.
It's because time is layered: some things make you sick
in certain periods, cause pleasure in others. Depends
on which layer you're struggling through. And when the results
are tallied, some are sheepish which should tell you something
about the way the world is run.

Just for a moment couldn't we doff the predatory guise?
Go back to the old landslide,
majority rule and similar outmoded pastiches of the truth?
I guess we'll each have fallen asleep separately
before the secret is out, the smallness of the universe and everything.
You'll call to me, won't you? I wouldn't want to sleep through
the Big Bang and miss the bus to work. You
will take care of me, won't you? Fuck, it's in both
our interests; the last chapter concerns me as much as anyone
and there's a lot to get done between here and the chasm—
pretending to believe in the intelligence of a superior being and not
cracking up when the diminished workload rises like the sun in August.
We'll all hang around together for a while after that.
God doesn't expect a perfect score
most of the time, but sometimes the idea occurs:
What am I doing this for?
If not for love, then what?
To offer comfort to the dying?

Who are these people anyway?
I confess I'm easily vexed sometimes.
I came down from on high to work with you,
force you to be creative.
Mostly I get blank stares. It seems once
people have decided you're unusual, you're stuck
with the way you and they behaved.
Now I wouldn't go so far as to call myself omnipresent—hell,
a lot of them have done that, and look where it gets them—behind the
    notions counter,
or as floorwalkers in the great department store of heaven.
"Fourth floor: rare anxiety, eternal ligaments. Sorry,
depression is in the basement. Watch your step please."

This concerned Rinty in a kind of way.
He and Rex had been friends—well, pals—for quite a while now.
They would pal around together in a certain way.
But their true connection to each other was through Kane.
He'd pat one of them, talk softly to him.
It seemed then that life on the ranch or behind the lines was very
    heaven.
Or it'd be: "Rex, you sonofagun! What's that you got there
in your fangs? Come on now, cough it up."
At which the obedient pooch would deposit a length of twine near his
    master's boot.
The real test came though when Rinty found Kane all tied up like that.
In a flash he knew what to do—chew through the cords so Kane could
    reach his holster,

and nary a moment too soon—the Gestapo guy returned
to the cell. "Vell, haf you considered the terms of my—"
Whop! in a moment Rinty was all over him, Kane kicked over the
    bales
of straw and ignited them and escaped through the door with Rinty
to the tunnel the Gestapo guy had left open, slamming the door
    behind them.
Now he was free to rejoin his twin brother,
he of the gorgeous tweeds, in the sky, in an airship floating over Paris.

How we like to recall these adventures! They make us interesting
to the girl next door who had just finished shopping and needs help
    with her groceries.
"Here, allow *me*," Kane proffered. Rinty saw it was unequal,
the match, and slunk off under the step.
And that's the way I'd like you to remember me, Lily,
though I know I have no say in the matter.
"Why you surely do, and that darling dog of yours. What's his name?"
"Rinty," Kane mumbled, abashed. "Short for Rin Tin Tin."
"*Ah, Rin Tin Tin—*
c'est connu, ça."

Beg pardon I don't speak much French.

A Hard Man

Soon the war would be over.
There would be April in Paris, sad
with the foreknowledge that all this was coming to pass.
How do you get out of it? I mean, there's a job to be done
and not much you can do to get out of it. Besides,
would one want to? As April is succeeded, daintily, by May
with hawthorn and crabapple blossoms
and a feeling that you're going to throw up, though you never do of
    course.
That would be conduct unbecoming to a hero of your stature
which is pretty far up there. No, everything's like new.
He jams his fist into his forehead. Not quite everything, it seems.
Toolkits will shrink and screwdrivers lose their bearings
ere he, the desired, detested enemy comes with good tidings,
and until that happens everything is ruined,
pitiful, gnawed. Some other year, maybe,
out of the parade of them, each with its majorettes
and streamers, but not today. You've guessed it. He's passed out.
    Again.

The President's Dream

Tourists assemble beneath the vast diorama.
It's time for father's ghost to be wheeled out again.
In shirtsleeves, as though not afraid of pity or rebuke,
the amorphous shape passes on its way in no time at all.

A woman weeping amid the tambours of some columns.
A dog at first attentive to its master,
bored later. Birds pester us with messages.

Shitty trips no one takes any more.
Sibyls scarcely consulted
and rarely believed. Can we take their irrelevance seriously?

All along it was coming to be dawn,
negotiating the furniture and cigar smoke
left from last night's set of variations.
Curtain shuddered delicately and withdrew.

* * *

Kane was a righteous dude, heat-packing.
Cared nor for right or wrong,
rode east, rode west. "Home's best," he smiled.
But indeed, where was home? Some place
under the sky's petals, attuned to harmony?
He preferred the poetry of Charlotte Mew to that of Nathalia Crane,
sang in the shower while the radio poured discord
about not believing in the Bible, or in hell, more precisely.
Heaven's chancy if you're saving someone
from evil's clutches, less so if you're not thinking
about anything in particular, on a day
just like the others, receding like cumulus
into the forever. He was damned if he knew.

He liked the smell of horseshit and sagebrush,
chaparral. Went about his business
with really nothing to spare left over.
Nobody ever knew if he got horny
or didn't let on if they did. Louise
would ask him, "Why don't you come in?
Those Nazis aren't coming back, since you smashed them."

To which he'd reply, "Better to stay on guard for the simple things
that defy the imagination, sift through it
like chaff through cornsilk. Oh, I'll
just stay on here awhile, I guess."

Now there were loud ones clouding up again,
ready to erupt in a furious squall
when the guard's attention was diverted by a stray
jackrabbit or other sign of activity,
even mental. The sky was dark as coagulated blood.
"Halleluljah! They must think I'm daft
not to notice what's going on behind.
Here, I think I'll fake a snooze, and then . . ."

These were to be his last words for some time.
The BBC operator scowled, then softly cursed.
It was a dark day for Bletchley. Wait, though—
through the crackle and hiss a voice could just be made out—
"Avast, ye slobs! *Espèces d'ordure!*"
Then all was silence again, silence of the English Channel

and the map room of the Imperial War Museum.
In a cellar somewhere in Paris the scratchy sounds
of the TSF had made their point, though. "We'll be coming
out of this just as soon as fate allows.
Meanwhile, patience and strength must be our watchwords."
He smiled, expiring faintly. The Nazis grinned and were glad.
Soon it would be time to break out the champagne again.

Kane was lost in the Métro,
somewhere between Plaisance and Pernety.

Far from others he assuaged a certain need,
felt better for it; the treetops and stars
danced and dwindled, from gateway to lounge.
Blandest of ghouls, the sergeant
thought to turn the situation to his advantage yet again.
"Born in Milwaukee, I grew up in central Illinois
with little to show for it. My college education
left much to be desired. Life in Montmartre
was 'twice as nice.' Lord forgive me
for the occasional breach of bathroom etiquette.
I soldier on."

Memories of misbehavior
were still fresh in their minds. They puzzled over a chart
thought to be of importance.
Boys and girls came out to play,
a little indifference goes a long way

toward the coquetry of the sublime. This delightedness
under the summer sky is theirs, if they but want it
really and truly. "The moon doth shine as bright as day,"
after all.

And then they die.
And then they keep on dying.
And then said nothing more.

Chapter Seven

The bloody creeps of war were not long in bringing an isolation to
this spot. Then I guess more visited it. It was not a sacred place, yet it
was in the sense that it was a place of pilgrimage. Rex and Rinty re-
membered it, Rinty perhaps a little more clearly due to his dog's dis-
position. Then I guess the others caught up with them, a few at a time.
The war was almost over now. You could tell because of the green light
in the evening sky. Mme. Delaunay brought out the redingote she'd
knitted before the war and placed it sideways on a chair, it caught the
sun's declining rays. It was a wondrousness of zigzags interrupted by
broken arcs toward the bottom and what looked like shards of tufa set-
tling haphazardly in the comforting environment of the broken arcs.
Long had she labored to sculpt the thing into something like distinc-
tion, but it had always seemed drab to her despite the profusion of
spring-like color that drenched it and the surrounding walls of the
room. She could see down into the tiny square that was almost dark

now, though up above the sky was light. A few vagrants trespassed, for what purpose it was hard to make out. There was a urinoir at the far edge from which men emerged quickly every so often, hastening their steps as the sheaf of light from the arc lamp troubled them. The war was dark and dense, but small now.

Yet it couldn't be ignored, not completely. It was there like the beginning of a migraine, the song of a siren leading to no good, but was beautiful in a kind of way that had been formal before the war, like the stiff invitation cards called bristol the postman would deliver. They always seemed too large for what they were used for. That kind of patriotism had blent with the ensuing informality and become a grave tempest, semi-formal as the invitations used to say. Marlise remembered one evening being driven far out into the country to what turned out to be a truck farm, or looked like one. There were no guards which was surprising but a kind of factotum, a young lout who did the honors, steering them toward the narrow corridor at the back to where the lettuces were stored. It seemed too late to begin, yet the melodious strands of dance music floated outward, a little livelier each time. To clasp this!

The Mist Rolls in from the Sea

I remember. It was one of those quite festive, forgotten afternoons. It never rains in southern California. Tin lizzies were slamming around the neat suburban streets in the Harold Lloyd movie, past lawns and houses that looked newer than 1923. They bespoke the quite pleasant ease of the suburbs, thinking of starting up a business. There was pandemonium down the street next to the drugstore with its soda fountain and the new dry-cleaning establishment. Whatever will we do, Eloise wondered. What will the neighbors think. That's easy, the neighbors don't think. Yes but my dress is ruined, the one I bought at the May Company—the cleaner let the iron scorch it. You better run out and pet your little dog. Please let me know. And I will try the mustard thing. How many others in their death before me. It is invited to be there. You're probably not supposed to die. Yet. The old Gimme bird fixed me with an angry socket. You must leave it. But I didn't favor it. Princess Hello plans to overwork you for four days a week.

I did advise these to leave me. Nothing more was said for several months. Then like a bee one has to swat it was August again. The policeman hailed a taxi. He was just checking. The sheriff loves those little bonbons. This is not a product, it is something different, like mice. Yet these things last forever. The parents of schoolchildren like them. And then didn't use it as much as he thought he was going to. You could, if you wished, have chosen another striped antenna.

Leave it to the lost rangers; they enjoy that. They walked away from it.

Dog Overboard!

Why haven't I told you? Here, it's your mess, you finish it. Americans are everywhere in America and some other places, though in lesser quantities, like when you're longing for somebody and that person longs for you, but for that to happen may be different. That other dark day, eleven years ... Other days will be chilly. Strange bugs appear.

All's a revival, she said. Some four-flusher may try to pinion you in the garden. Pay no attention, it will unbalance his pretence. Yet you had no business being there. His love will be of some use, to him, but of short duration. The cloud-like fingers will materialize over the recycled water. And I've got to go. Down there some dog may be fighting for his life. I'll risk that, take a chance on leaving you until the dusk comes again with its secret aromas. There is no time for meddling. How I wish I could take you with me to the piano, but one of us has to stay here; the other must guard the precinct. Excuse me? The instinct, I meant to say, the others must gasp at their instincts and will be gone tomorrow too. Like a gipsy's painted cart the future trails off into the distance, useless. Useless as a barking dog, the meow of a cat, closing in on this chapter, vibrant once. Threaded now.

Dog and Pony Show

As Pussycat stept out of the house, a black dog she hadn't seen before came around the corner. Now the wind calls to some; others are asleep. The worm sleeps in the swamp.

A Lost Dog

Dominge satisfait alla trouver son Maistre à Agien, dans un jeu de paume,
avec Laverdin, qui quitterent la partie pour l'interroguer. Cestuici parla de
cest affaire avec des loüanges de son Capitaine, non si eslevees, mais plus
judicieuses que celles de Bacouë, et de ce coup perdit entierement l'amitié
se son Maistre et la recompense de trente-huit harquebusades qu'il avoit sur
luy. Marquez à quoy eschappent les grands, voire les meilleurs.
—AGRIPPA D'AUBIGNÉ, *Sa vie à ses enfants*

Sniffing contentedly along the Miracle Mile, unlike some, adjusting the seam of her stocking in front of the plate-glass window of a black and white candy store, Rinty saw her go over to the other side of the street and drop something in a mailbox. Could it be that she was one of those women who don't like dogs? No, for she half-smiled at him, meanwhile muttering something like "We've got to find out what's in that sarcophagus!" An open roadster driven by a man in a checked cap pulled up at the curb. Evidently the woman knew him for she walked over to the car across the narrow strip of grass between the sidewalk and the street. "No, nowhere ... Nothing special." She smiled at the man and gave him a conspiratorial wink. Rinty was trembling. "He hides his face to become an evil spirit," she explained. "The medicine gourd is my sister Betty's, and the axe is the sign of Skip, the thunder god."

As the witch doctor danced, he began to chant and wail. His voice rose to a hideous shriek as he hopped about. "That caterwaulin' alone could scare the wits out o' any critter," Rinty reflected.

In the fullness of time a foolish man did a good thing.

They walked rapidly behind the hound, who kept his nose to the ground, with ears flapping. He stopped beside the steps of a small trailer. It was weirdly painted in psychedelic colors.

My Own Best Customer

Bronze building borders chafe at the cat's slow progress. They told us it would be slow but not this slow. It was Mother's Day or Father's Day, with stuff sifting from the trees as in autumn, but from no particular branch, one couldn't even be sure of seeing the stuff or inhaling it. From the silence it began to be evident that many of us ought to stop and consider what might be gathering in the crotches of trees, perhaps ready to lash down at us. But one's attention was attracted by a thin parade of go-getters.

Thus it happens that a mere-photo-op happens to be there standing in for the real thing, whatever that might be, then becomes the real thing. Unanswered letters and unreturned calls stand up and cheer: it is their grief that is being measured, and in that they are able at long last to rejoice. Gradually the hiatus comes to be peopled with things like real characters in a real field. The cat and various dogs are ground into the wings like ash into a carpet. Someone lights a spill and touches it to the asbestos curtain. A disaster unlike any other in history could be brewing. Then we remember that all disasters resemble each other. They are monochrome, a field of mud to be tracked into history's temple. Oh if only our childlike selves could see us and comment on us now, wouldn't we be grateful for the blur and the spots of grease floating on the soup's surface. *Now*, it would seem, word might have reached the outpost and backup be on the way. Sure enough, a posse gallops through so fast that nobody's quite sure what happened.

The dogs of yesterday are tomorrow's children, they have the same faces and mannerisms, the same underarm hair. The same telltale differences of detail in their worn tunics and leggings; the same cruel, abruptly stifled laughter coming from the next room. All the goddesses wanted you to wear these. Therefore make nice, the pageant's nearly over. A single crinkled brown leaf floats in midair for what seems like forever. Go home, children, it is time. Other incidents will excite you barely five minutes from here, but for now it seems the period has truly ended. Go back to your homes, up to your rooms, anywhere as long as it's quiet around you. In the interim big pieces of furniture will flash, oxidized. Happening will be out of harm's way, but so, alas will the dislocations that propel living, turning us good one moment, naughty the next; the variety will have worn off and there'll be nothing left to do. We will be BORED.

If it's life, it's *real* life. It's all about sex, isn't it? The night before, amusingly he had taken off his pants and folded them up before getting into bed. The dreams—of being in the subway, lost, yet unable to not proceed toward some thoughtful goal. He could never stop taking chemistry and now, as to that theology . . . Sex roars back at me, like a vengeful but toothless lion. Some day I am going to write about that.

If only what between me and you
never happened. Listen,
it looked very different in those days,
in a truck back from Texas, a few elder
suits commented the
divisiveness, for the umbrella specialized.
Oh, we're not floating at all.
Desserts, too, have gone through the roof.
You say one thing, it all bunches up.
We sat on it and jerked it.
I'm ready. I'm ready too.

That one you loved, the great cat, so pure in ethos, is she, is she too not around any more? Like dancing in Jerusalem, man. From each door a household emerged and stood watching us as we marched along the street. Other days are bone-dry. This was an almost perfect specimen. Kane watched as the other men pushed through. It sounded like a merry-go-round but we imagined it. The shy horse's face was full of vigor now. He'd catch the mountain lion in an open contest. Yea, and three seers would be here under the trees to throw down scraps of praise on him. But we must tread lightly here. This is where time enters into the equation. You don't feel up to it. But his gaze, clear as through speckled glass, goes on and on, a thing of wonder to us. I feel as though I know how the ancients slid across the moraine until something in the air made them stop. The holiness emptied of special things, dishes and utensils that are no more, are not to be, like the very stars which are extinct long before their light reaches us, causing us to sigh and purse our lips. They held a counsel and decided to push on above the rock line if that is what had to be. There is something innately courageous I think in this ignorant attitude. It puts its stamp on the scene as far as the remote horizons. Oh what am I going to do if the attitude turns out wrong, as so often, if I should have been back *there*, waiting not letting on to the others about my suspicions and concerns, even if it put them in danger, drew them stealthily into the dog's trap. Unfortunately there is no one who can advise you on these things—no one whose advice you'd be willing to take, anyways. Me and Buster, we—

Life should be simple and fashionable. Writing novels and shit is a way to gain a living. A gay clown was there, looking for work? And if the stripped franchises no longer work for you, who's to say they're any better than you? I thought—I mean I was going to have a cup of coffee. The welter of spring came in. This gentleman over here'll have two. I lost a pair of my mother's friends and said a prayer; they appeared before me veiled as in a dream. You smelled it for thirteen cents. *The Big Clock*, *The Big Knife*, and *The Big Sleep* were all playing, next to *The Big House*. Still, if you'd rather I'd . . .

Octavia seemed to take this lightly, but behind her normally regal bearing were what I supposed were lost action figures. She was disappearing down oblivious paths, one from another, that came together in the sea like the stains of a shipwreck. She needed nothing less to proclaim a *congé*, as she called it. Everyone was to leave these premises for what would turn out to be quite a long time, in fact. Those who had no place to go were the least worried. They sang and smiled, touching foreheads as in the other time. It was the predestined who seemed to be in a state of shock, not wanting to talk about it but issuing evident distress signals. "Access—hello?" It seemed there was no one at home but it turned out to be just another deceptive habit of seeming; in fact there were plenty of people in the front hall, some of them backing up the stairs. Octavia's gaze swept the cretonne-clad throng. "Well, you haven't answered my riddle yet." Her eyebrows were imperial but in fact her voice was but barely audible. Was she having a change of heart? Would I get a chance to drive a few of them home after all? Of course I couldn't appear eager or even interested or the whole project might have been dashed against the rocks. "Well," she sighed wearily after a certain time, "I suppose some of you can go. Much that doesn't depend on you will be happening here soon." She swept sideways into one of the antechambers. I saw that my chance had come. No one here was going to remember any of this for very long.

I thought it odd—but what do I know? It's very pretty if you look down in back of the house what they thought. It's got this weird stuff in it. Lady comes in with a ladder to be fixed. I say lady (porch door?), by the time you got into the right angle with it our next piece of truth is a painted fjord. Do they still deliver? *All right, John. John are you home?* I am a pack rat. This they chew into a paste and place it under a neighbor's tongue. To be rid of the deliciousness, what a relief! I can do without a little of the prank of the mirroring ritual. It puts people off. Sometimes for days, weeks on end. Go put it away—like eggs on a tray.

Both had a long and sleepy history. One came from where it had been aroused. Now, there was no place. A phantom fort. If history let it go (if it was gone from history) we were released—but into whose custody? The trample-headed? No one can go up there, in wider arcs. That's about it. The losses are stars, like puzzling sharks. As it is now, there are no visas, or they are unlearned. Three times seven times he circled the uniform walls, and it was all as if in snow but without the thunder of unloving. I heard someone else say: Doesn't anything change in these parts? NEVER! Think of it as a minor chord, a distinction—or don't. Not everything has to pretty-please heaven, and we're several versts from even that, pun intended. Kane came to this wilderness before Crawford thought of it, yet it was he would later be set up as a victim, of his own freewheeling, selfish ways, lusting after a piece of darkness worthy of its locus. And long after he and Kane had parted ways the conviction persisted that neither had seen the other. Yet how could that be? They were postulated on the same plane, and adults had seen them. Rex was almost certain of that. But how to distinguish between sincerity and feigned sincerity? There is the problem. Kane thought he could distinguish from the wearer's expression whether he was telling the truth or not. But with animals it's a completely different ball game. Suppose Rex was out to deceive him. How could he tell? The nag's muzzle always looked pretty much the same, whether he was pawing the straw in his stable or rubbing his head appreciatively against Kane's arm after a treat of some sort. Rinty always looked attentive, jaws open, tongue a-pant, with a kind of serious, alert smile, and then his ears would prick up. But who can sound the depth of feeling in an animal's skull? It could be they were both out to get him, were in league with Crawford and Crawford's men. There would be nothing to warn until the final moment when the bullet popped out. No use then to ask, Rinty, what are you doing there? *Et tu, Rex?* The truth comes out only at the end, when everything has happened. But then more things happen, and what may have been not true turns out to be true, or everything will get so scattered around that no sense can be made of it. Perhaps there never was any, after all. Indeed.

Dog of the Limberlost

With a can of spray-dust
a walk is easily taken
on the leaves of the book laid powerfully parallel
though this book isn't the storehouse of might
you dreamt up in the middle of the storm-tossed night
where tattoos end in particulars evaporating
in a kind of silence that continues on above
chimney pot and shards of roof
on that particular fall.
Seven hedges encircle the man who is dancing
to the tune of an eternal bug-eyed conception
not one of his ancestors knew about
any more than he
the one doing the dancing
amid others becomes part of the dance
welling up to his hips.
The radio was on.
Some of the men were listening
and began to do an idle dance
below the ceremonial that is prepared.

One animal received the presentation.

I listened to it on the radio
wondering why nothing stops the serial
free to go on inventing itself
through fire through thunder through blisters of time
and the world. Nothing much comes to cheat us
of this vapor.

Cheese—at the moment? Nutcases.
The night when you saw Screwy Squirrel
When I went over to him I said I'm sorry.
We respect these.

William Biggs died some years ago.

Sex on the River

> *The Mayor is urinating on the wrong side*
> *of the street! A dandelion sends off sparks:*
> *beware your hair is locked!*
> —JAMES TATE, "The Wheelchair Butterfly"

Methought the King of Thule
sat by my side in the empty banquet hall,
a gilded goblet in his hand. "Here, try some of this.

It'll put lead in your pencil." "No thanks, King."
Like a madman he staggered to the balcony,
tossed the thing into the sea.

Spring came and went so fast this year.
The rookies one that year.
Not one to beat about the bush, rootless,
roofless I go on.

I pick up the chosen advice
like broken watchworks—will it be time for me?
Or for some other—

"Conflict of interest, I'm afraid.
He declined to represent me." The old man spoke no more.
We were out of time,
had to be leaving
on a new desperate adventure.
If only we could believe it.

Where shall we meet up afterward?

A Long and Sleepy History

Ma chambre a la forme d'une cage.
—GUILLAUME APOLLINAIRE, "Hôtel"

Act so that there is no use in a centre.
—GERTRUDE STEIN, *Tender Buttons*

Never ones to beat about the bush, they cut to the chase, came to un-surprising conclusions. The purple headdress is at rest now. At least there is no one to see us. We may be glad, under the sheaves of sun and an impertinent river runs up to your door. "My, how opportune." Stepping into the little skiff one is quickly carried away to a land of impatient dreams. No, it's this way we wanted to come. Nobody wanted to lie down. The daughter of Dr. Jekyll passed by slowly, against the iron palings of the little park. A smile was on her lips but we could not see. A little dog followed closely, sniffing to see what it was all about. The scene was repeated once exactly, and not again.

The man who sells orange papers walked by, wailing, his arms burning. It was not quite the right time of day, then he too went away, his perp walk fading into the cladding that surrounds the houses here in this northern capital. "I *am* a pack rat," one said, as though to reassure him-self. Then he too disappeared diagonally, down to the port from which explorers set out to discover the New World every so often. My, but it was dusty under the trees. A trickle of water from the parched foun-tain, and . . .

Sometimes they tell you not to walk in a certain way. In this they are right, for one should walk one way, no way in particular, but it should be the same at all times. That is why I am here. You notice that I'm not walking any more. If I were, I should be somewhere else. This is the place it pleases me to be, placed within the animated buzz of the barkless tree. All life and all limes are like this. We picked it up from each other, carried it a little ways, set it down like a pail of water that was too heavy and slopping over. Then some other person sidled, offered to help. Why not, after all? And by now we had come a good distance together. The red skiff was still anchored there, it had not grown any smaller. The laws of perspective never play tricks on you, it just seems that way from the new distance above the scene that stays as flat as ever. No, we could never play tricks with cheeses, and now the hands have gone to bed. The dear girls were ripe for resting, and in this magical glade rest seems to occur rather naturally. All the colors at once are a relaxing credo too. The hands are placed just that way, along your back. It must be great to lay that way and always lying down, waiting for the mood to come. The mood *will* come, meanwhile you'll be too relaxed to deal with it immediately, but it always stays around temporarily and then there is a use for it, a time to do something with it before the other sleepers return. You who worship us, lay that liquid feather on the ground. The ground, the sky must be some use, or the air would vanish. But it stays in place, like shellac on a counter. Please, turn the heavy page. Be raw and muddy.

A few more moments and the wreath of cares is done.

Dena's mother was sound asleep. And Chauncey told me that story back in the 1940s. Drew and Harris are disarmed. Organ meats are served to the invited guests. Brighteners are needed. There wasn't a dry ice in the house. At the end only a few of them came back on stage to take the traditional bow. The whereabouts of the others was a mystery and remains so to this day. Except for me, of course, and even I am not sure I can explain it to you. I was clutching an old bag of zinnias so as to have something to carry, so as not to look foolish. Next to me an actress who played Lady Godiva nudged her mount forward, pulling on its bit so the poor beast's head dodged up and down. This was cruel. And of course the applause was frantic. Nothing like a naked lady and a beast of burden to bring down the house, so to speak. And it was brought down. In the dust and confusion children screamed for their parents, husbands sought their wives, many of them undistinguishable under the black or yellow dominos they had been given to wear. In the end though it seemed everyone was accounted for. That was the moment I found myself outside, on the little triangle of grass that separated the stage door from the vast cream-colored marquee whose opalescent lights trembled in the blue evening air, for it was still light, the summer solstice was still on. I thought I heard someone call me by name. "Norman ... ?" But it was an illusion, like all the other illusions that had paraded past us that endless, decisive evening. "Barbara ..." My lips started to form the word and then thought better of it. I knew Barbara was at home, probably reading or asleep by now. "BARBARA?" The voice began like thunder, pulling itself up into a cloudlike shape, then expiring for what seemed like hours, with something like tact, though this was not the time for it.

If only I had studied a little harder I might recognize the next chapter. We might have known each other, been known. Still a little goes a long way I guess when we are talking about everything. So we might not have known about ourselves. As it was we guessed we knew each other and that was enough for that time in our life, a ripe day.

What a collision everything tried to make itself into, when especially water comes rolling down the hill toward us. It is perhaps wiser steeply to ignore such decisions made on behalf of others, till they become part of us and we may sweep no more. Thrice toss these oaken ashes in the air. It was only a bridal slump but everything becomes permanent after a few minutes.

The other time was when he purposely stayed out late, phoning in every half-hour or so, until finally I became distracted and went to bed. A certain triangular sleep like the corner of a pillowcase veils the sugared parting, chews on how we went to bed. Sleep is the better for the drip of disorder that persists *en filigrane* in that snowy wall, a white shed containing tools both useless and necessary until you get up and find the noise really was a burglar after all! Now there's a state of things! But you've got to ignore your mother's pushing, focusing on what she's really like as well as the smaller occurrences that are sprinkled along every path's edge, the "seam" of seem. Then other proposals are tabled to be made of what we may, the flounce not adorable, the trailing laces under suspicion, and the wide inspection is made as economically as possible, the feasibility study becomes suddenly feasible. If only we had been left alone on a certain day in a particular house but that's another story of course. I bid you good night.

Someday I swear I'm going to . . . No, but what was he saying? Something about chain lightning, how certain dudes grind it out regardless? How there is lightning in winter too, sometimes? It was going to be time to seek shelter soon. It would be getting dark. Already it wasn't as light as a little while ago, when it was difficult to make out the stone letters of the church facade. Something about how we should always be kind and grow with one another to the end that comes as naturally as breath. The greenest lay is the hardest to sing. The last breath is the easiest to draw. Ruse of knights and ladies, overheard but not yet seen, and then the sweetest memory, perhaps the earliest one, is abruptly yanked away, for you can never know how far you have come, only how much distance is left to scrape along in an uninteresting manner. If only I had the secret! But one can't be the sin and the sinner simultaneously, or it works out that way, sometimes a pitcher of milk is all there is. Away with those who trust us! We have brighter things to blind us. Now is never. It saves us for the sacredness of talk.

My son was born yesterday. No, it only seems that way. He has been around for many years, since my earliest childhood in fact. He speaks but says little. He is as the lining to my coat. We never see each other, and there is no distance between us. Once we were on a golf course and he said, "Dad, why are those men hitting those little balls. Why doesn't God punish them?" Another time we were running around in the dark, downtown, and I truly understood him for once, understood the meaning of a scream. It's not at all what you might think, it's like the fuzzy inside of a peach or an apricot. Nothing gets to be a no-starter without a little help from the decor of pink rosebuds and cupids; the end is all too near. Little wonder there are not many takers for the conclusiveness that erupts then.

A listener told me not to "worry" about perceived injustice. "Build me a hill," he commanded. Very dirty children were paid eleven dollars and sixty cents an hour. In a month the thing was done. It wasn't a bad hill, just not particularly engaging looking. When one thought of climbing it one's thoughts immediately turned elsewhere. After a while it became all but invisible, in the sense that nobody ever seemed to notice it. One could drive by or even over it without the idea of it ever grazing one's fancy. But he called it a fine hill. It must have been all the labor that went into it, but even more that it was useless, as faceless a feature of the landscape as existed then in those parts. Oh, I don't wonder. Does landscape really count? What is it for? What is it? Some of them has to have all the add-ons, plug-ins, to make of this a gracious house. I say it matters but it doesn't matter all that much. There, I've finished. You can have your say now. For each separate house.

Say silence is a broken record. We are the drum-taps of its affabulations. Rex knew this, but just wandered away. Into a bunch of trees close by. They came looking for him urgently, but not until after a lot of time had elapsed. He was gone by then. Hell, anybody would be even if they hadn't gone anywhere. Which is why Rex kind of liked the situation he had all unwittingly caused. Nobody could say greed was involved in it, or any other human passion. It was merely erased, like so much of time, what time takes with it. Now Rinty was affected by it too. Not so most people would notice, but just the way in which he hung around the cabin tipped those in the know. Was he unhappy? Morose? Happy? Hard to say, unless you were down there with him, close to the boards, and even then. Nobody had a word for what he or they were thinking. This went on into the hereafter.

Meanwhile, the attention of the Americans was caught by a herd of lyre-horned Ankole cattle grazing on the grassy slopes.

"Right smart-lookin' beeves," Chow commented.

The Quitter

I began to relax, and succeeded so well that certain
friends became concerned. "What is this roller-coaster
of moods you've been subjecting us to lately," one
inquired. Well, it's not me, I swear. Certain pauses
lead to entropy in nothing flat. If you're caught out
on the airstrip it's conceivable you wouldn't notice
anything unusual. On the dank straw of a dungeon,
it becomes something quite different. "We knew you
were one of us when your sister came over." Well,
that's right, but it's not right. What amazes me is the lack
of a clue or anything resembling one, or
even an inkling such things can exist. Look, I'll
square with you. Five hours ago I was not what I am now.
That's ancient history to me. I dimly remember eating an orange
and the world changing. That's all I want to say now.
Eventually I'll be issuing a public statement
but for now all I want to do is rest. And consider.

Sometimes it's enough just to believe in what could happen,
and sometimes, to question that it ever could.
You and I are walking down a street together,
suddenly one of us isn't there. Or it's a street in winter,
it was never there. The truth and the means to oust it
never existed. Someone knew it was warm in there,
another never heard of the situation, or a similar one.
Sometimes it takes two not to believe in

the affability of an aging present,
while at others along comes the serpent, the mess
to be mopped up. You see there was no other one of us
there, only us, not enough to frighten or make a difference,
but the curving sandbar always suggests another time, a
    re-engagement.

More about Drew

Bright confusion reigned in the hillocks and ravines. Ulysses rubbed his eyes, lurching up the old path, half-certain he was home. The but half-remembered scenery is intensely replicas. That whole area was sealed off. But is it safe? Put padlocks up in trees, turn on wind machine, imitate coughing sounds. The lake responded with a distant glitter, which could throw us off jewels forever, once the file is opened. He was subtly careful now. Those clogged dossiers can lie active for hundreds of years, ready to dart out like a rattlesnake at the sound of a falling leaf. But is it info? All he knew was he wanted some grub and a shower and a place to bunk down for the night. Not so fast, my man, the voice clacked idly from behind, or was it? Who knew where the offering had come from, whose hands had soiled it. Best to leave it be, even if not a booby trap there will be others come dialing time. Not to infer catastrophe from a dance frieze, at the same time not let evildoers off the hook.

Modern Sketch

Sleep a weak hour
in the sense of right now
You're not gonna believe this
air of Reynaldo Hahn:
"C-est l'heure ... l'heure exquise"—sho'!

He taught me to masturbate,
for which I'll always be grateful, and
about how sounds sound
boiled to perfection

Why must we complicate everything
about your coming over.
I said your coming over
throw money at the rat.

Otherwise than us is nothing
left in the empty wilderness.
I'll always be grateful
the wind chides in a corner

It was around bookish park
no one can go.
Nobody can go in.
This are is off limits.

When they come back to chase you
all that will be left is a little pile of pins.
No more than nine.
Now I'll be left to sweep out the house.

It was getting darker and
going to rain. Everybody was forced
to leave the area. No snake-repellent.
Other than that it was endure,

endure some more, come on.
You must know where you left it.
It is exactly where you left it.
I want out. I've
never played this game before
and I want out. And so you shall, my bonny—OUCH!
my bonny lass. We have come to the head of the trail.

It stinks like a pin.
Oh tell me—but no one can tell me,
it is true. No one
knows the way to the weatherizer.
Four women before me failed.
Will be nowhere wiser.
The fifth can't salute.

If so, why bother
sober ascending

Apple Annie

The great war and the troubles that went alongside
it were as quick silver eddies on the
forest floor of Evan's life.
We too had jabbered, not urgently, but sure
the mouse was come along.
Under the bed, the rain and all the dust cast off
to make a show, sport of itself
as though minions of the past were past
believing the forge of corners
dissolute with disbelief.
The four matrons hurried forth.
There was not to be another assembly
then, or ever.
So much it was sure.

And when some savaged the dark basketball cliffs
too much ire drew on themselves
were forced to fall back.
No one does it like you do, she said, sweetie, honey,
father of my children. You can just
take that off
place it over the silver tip of a chair
back to the light
back to the light it says.

When the father tethered the sloop to a twig
near shore, the unintended consequences
exploded risible. There was more sauce to pour,

a devil of a half-hour moon.
Pretty soon it came on with motivations
for all those in the offing,
those who commanded a sizable identity
in the plaid milieus of where they first
heard what it means to be going about lone
with blisters for everyone.
The necklace scratches. I'll return it to the rightful owner
if I can find him (hee, hee). Or turn to crepe
in the dusk-dawn of day, same as every while
at every tip the lorded lark explodes
with the factory whistle in her darkling eyes. Drab pots.

To Meet with My Father

As I walked on amid fires, a young man approached. "Lots of dry cool places—May I lie along it?" He seemed disturbed, nestled. Just so far could he go. Bud looked up in amazement. The woman was just leaving. She had been overseas.

Why pursue others' habits with ethereal woes? The pinprick of not doing anything hurts worse than what is by the fireside. Ben came to realize this. In his whole life was only two moments where he could speak his piece and spoke it rather well.

Narielle had other fish to fry just then. A cabinet meeting next door. All the men going in, plus the token saints to be dusted, and there was a rather brisk smell of bacon. Bud and Lucas would rather have it that way. As for her, there wasn't much of anything she didn't like. She just didn't like people hanging around and dropping in on some pretext. After all it was much too late for that. Or so Uncle Possum opined.

* * *

I liked the fourth declension—all those "u"s. So much of Latin, till then, was "x"s and "v"s—like Roman architecture, or Rome itself. Cicero and Petronius. Cornelia and her jewels. Always a frontal verticality, or horizontal woolgathering philosophy of the old school. But the fourth declension—and the ablative absolute—is one of those surprises destined to appear regularly throughout the Roman experience. Similar are the famous "mustard fruits" of Cremona. A delicacy? I think not. But a conversation stopper, definitely, that makes you go back over the recent distance, the liquid recent past like water as evoked by Debussy. Not to worry. Not to shudder. Better things—though not the best—may be lurking around the next corner, or it may be "Go to Jail." Forget the hotel on Kentucky Avenue. This isn't living, either, but maybe a larger segment of some still unmapped, vaporous continuity. We can live with that, right? And if not, you can always scrap it. Indifferently reflective, half-informed by an ageless glitter, he makes his way to the lectern, harassed by bigwigs, cheered on by schoolgirls. In what a joyless world we evolve it's a wonder we find time for pets and hobbies, not undone by prophecies, or not this time, but be careful, God is the crossing guard. You wouldn't want him to interrupt you.

So the Emperor's clean clothes are brushed and folded and placed without undue reverence in the palissandre *crédence*. He whose chiefest pleasure it was to "fart through silk" has been violently reconstituted in another hemisphere, awaiting the kangaroo-court's pleasure while the clock ticks patiently by, marking the hours "in intent." If he had understood the significance of that phrase when, as a three-year-old, he held chickweed out to the expectant robins, expecting something himself, the glass might not have sunk so low. It is a mean time we live through, expected to cover for the commanding officer whose lunch break has extended to an inordinate length. But we bow and gargle and carry our buttocks from one subcontinent to the other, delighted when anyone notices our absence, however brief. But the vast files haven't budged: like impassable moraines slowly absorbing the dark as the sky goes light, then fades behind them, creating a quizzical unbuilt architecture whose function only the absent ruler knows: like where the haha eases into the patient prairie beyond.

Miss Otis Regrets Land's End

We went to America, we didn't see what they were doing there. They don't drink pop. Too, I was a bride in the Thirties. B. Cellini meets A. Toklas. No, but I was going to wish him a happy Wednesday anyway. What if the ship sank? Would all this have gone on anyway? Medford or Medfield Oregon. The forest of siblings. Of sleep, a bunch. Dancin' when you're done. *Molto confortabile*, he suggested. And that's not nice! Country knockers! Is it ... a Broadway melody?

But I don't see how pushing. Tommy and Elfrida's case was different. There might be a thunderstorm must possess an interesting history. Oh captain restaurant, for the house! She can snow, but at 88 its tresses improbably implicate hers. He'll have had the honor.

In sappy bondage, I believe I might have been a pirate, once, by the bend in the river. It all comes down to this: fecal patterns. And growth pattern slugs. I probably ought to of, but cons override this, got herself a biker. What the, she's happy. And so arse we—just don't know it yet.

Several years ago I might have answered differently when asked the question: What abuts truth? Now we know we can make corners, distance is for the middle-aged. Chrysanthemums, thousands of them. And if you like it I'll toast some cheese, I knows you likes it. Aw, a fella comes on sheepish when you plan an outing and discard some shade, at the canyon's very lisp. And I thought you and me wuz . . . Drop it. There's no point in being younger about three guys. And now I believe you.

* * *

Are you trying to stop us? There you go. Oh, I don't wonder. New factors entered in. Hanging out with Baptists. It seemed. The words had an unpleasant ring. *The one* city. Oh I am sure it was as serious then to be struggling. On hill and vale was struggling and over all it was not anything near sensationalism. Just rain dripping into the barrel, something like that. Not easy, yet not too clear either, and do we need either of these, ever? At home the day begins early. 8AM and the phone is reading, somebody needing something, book left in the back of a car. Then breakfast, a pleasant interval in the day, with coffee and hot milk or orange juice. Time for a few wisps of conversation, then it's back to the chore that was abandoned a little while ago. Are there a lot more things to do? What is your opinion? Mostly it's the *getting back*, a chore like a sea wind and gulls coming to meet you, you'd hoped for more than this, or more comfort at least, but it's always a "gray area." We find what we come out to meet. All over the states states' rights are being handled and handled well too. So if all it takes is a little housekeeping, why not I say, so much the better if the end is to be avoided for a short while now. No bickering, let's have no more of that now. We can go back to being in the order of each other's beds, and the rugs beside them, and the chairs pushed against the bed to make a kind of steps leading to the floor—oh wasn't it like this last month and the one before that and the others stretching back into the coal dust of whatever it was doing before? It's only a matter of time before two handsome critics sink fingers of mush into whatever it is. As for finding more clues, the trail seems to have gotten suspiciously cold. There's the leaden echo and the golden echo, yes, but between these lie hundreds of leagues of uninspected, undefined terrain, sown with land mines as well as small, delicate flowers that should have come before, but, somehow, didn't.

Oh, we're not floating at all. We're partial home buyers and as such spend a lot of time on the floor, just lolling. We sat on it and jerked it. In the fullness of time a foolish man did a good thing. So's your Aunt Emma. These women are dangerous. I saw him holding the book in his hand. *Think Fast, Mr. Moto.* Other understanding of it, should that ever arise to the level of an occasion, or more be felt at another time, would process into the motes we already were. We needed only a hairy wrist for the flowers of time to carpet-bomb the whole way we had come, as wide and as deep-set as a glacier. Then—"good times." The prancing of tires on a frozen roadway, expecting to promise what we knew no random event could deliver. So we passed on, under the railroad overpass and various inscriptions. Suddenly dividing it into quarters seemed the proper response. The scene changed to a proper though barren bourgeois interior. Ducks were screaming on a nearby pond, perhaps caught in its frozen clutches. They know all about water, but ice is a rather different matter, I'll say. Then, though it was already late early evening, a young boy came around telling us all to go somewhere, somewhere not too far away but not a place we had heard of.

* * *

Nothing if found convenient. That good stuff just isn't there any more; it's even impossible to say for sure that it ever existed. That boy who looked adoringly at you twenty, thirty or forty years ago, with the gentle Kane Richmond eyes and licorice breath and the long, gently curved ass (envy of the other ranch hands) is a figure in another mythology whose parables know nothing of this world's. Do even they exist? Hard to say, everything being a matter of opinion anyway. Hey, that's your opinion. That's what I'm trying to say mate, perhaps in a language to which your inexquisite ears aren't attunded, but it's saying it, and generously too.

Mother will soon be here, fondling her pet Sealyham, wondering why no one lit the carefully laid fire. It will be time then to try and tell her what all this was about. All about us is ajar, like the door is or was the time you tried to break in, having lost your keys on some car seat. They're everywhere in the trees, madam! There is another inside another for another time.

There You Go!

Art always appealed to him. The way the strokes of brush go flying off the canvas, but stay around, watchful to the end. They appeal to what is best in us because they will fly away but still never go away. Oh I am sure it was as serious then to be struggling, those who stayed around knew it or gradually came to realize it. And there was fun in the trap of it. Art came pouring down on the listener, soothed his bandaged hands. The gentlefolk of the town dropped by from time to time. There was hooting in the bronze stairwell. No one was made to feel she had stayed too long, overstayed their welcome, that would be an impossibility since "welcome" was the whole world, how you felt about it and its wishing you well from time to time, so that it was impossible to say, "Excuse me, I think it's time to leave." All about you would be milling and streaming, rivers of Roman striped ribbons from cartwheel hats that say, "No, excuse us! Please, you be the guest." Rivers of ornamental charcoal burners and perspective studies, flawless most of them, put you in a good mood and then there's no place to find your hat. You don't need it, your hat! You're not going home. You're not going anywhere!

Kane felt the stubble growing across the back of his neck. That pretty June Lawson had been giving him the eye but pretending not to. The sort of person who when you go up to her stares at you and you remember to take your hat off and rub the nape of your neck and she'll say, "Oh, were you going somewhere?" "Shucks, I was, but I guess I'll stay now, or maybe I'll go, it's kind of getting to be time . . ." And she says, "Have you tried the cake?" and walks away, leaving you alone among a few stragglers and the trash that was starting to accumulate on the grass. Dang it all . . .

It could be a Chinese funeral for all the notice they were taking of each other. Each involved in a solemn gesture like a transparent jar, that left no room to speculate on where the others might have been left. It always comes as a shock to realize that there aren't any, that this was always a lonely place, not even created by God so you can't call it god-forsaken. Just like that, lonely and a little formal which stands out in such a wilderness the way a hitching post would stand out in the Gobi desert. You know it's not meant for you, for you to notice, but still, there's a hushed deliberateness about it that's not the same as the regular emptiness that passes slowly by like a conveyer belt with nothing on it, nothing to convey except the idea that this could be something if the light of the world would let it. And yet—there's a bee! A bunch of them, must be a whole storm of them come drifting in like the sea all of a sudden. And you are made to understand that the sea is someone's property, that everything belongs to someone even if that someone doesn't know about it, is unconscious or long dead and buried ages ago. Promise me sea, you'll reveal your owner's name? Oh, we, we're just waves, whatever they are. No belonging, no being. But the faint throbbing? That must be art, the kind that reveals nothing, no dead longings. Just a still-life a child might draw. But I thought the finished-art notion was supposed to stick around and be something, a hat or something. That's the enthusiastic part of it, imparts pep, makes you want to get up and leave. Yes, well, all right, it does do that, you're right, and so now it may be time for you to leave. You'll know, somehow. Yes, but the thinking part, I liked that. I kind of like to think about thinking. And so you shall, and you may never have to go anywhere. But I kind of like the idea of travel, gets you different places, you think about them and come back and you have had what I call an experience. The children's dresses may grow other places, topsy-turvy winds funnel the spruce branches. The library's stuck on a pile of steps too high for anybody to climb. Waves bang against the shore with a dreadful lack of enthusiasm. We could stay here and dream about these, but inasmuch as we have seen them it behooves us to stay here and reflect. Reflecting—isn't that the most important thing a human can do? Look at how a pond reflects trees—imperfectly, perhaps, yet as perfectly as it knows how, and the little mistakes in the reflection are what makes it charming and nice, gives stealth to what would otherwise be a random picture of choice. Surely this is the reason we are all drawn to art, and why art loves us, and if anything were any different, that is more or less perfect, it wouldn't have the same hold over us. What I mean is we can dream safely in our environment because art has set soft, invisible limits to it. This way we don't hurt ourselves, neither do we dream of unregulated schemas that might be beyond or outside us that might wish us no ill yet actually consume us one unguarded day. The afternoon, the hill, the ribbons, the kindly greeting of a passerby from a car, the library books to be collected and returned, they are sitting in the hall, the chill of a look of evil from a random child passing, the unspeakable number of houses that just go on mounting into the sky, the indifferent birds (and does each one have a nest?), the smooching and lovemaking that goes on on a mattress just above us, the tears and gentle crashing of the sea that really does mean it now and is sorry about having appeared indifferent before, the balcony that seems too big for the small hotel it's attached to, Mother's dress on the day they came to tell you it was time to get dressed, they were taking you to the city, there was a small chance you might never return, the cauliflowers and potato bugs, the whole heap of music that in time will reduce all this to an orderly pile of dust ... Oh, it's just too much to stand! I know that, but you must stand here and stand it.

What if they came by and saw us? What would people think?

* * *

Why wait for another day to cross itself? For what is revealed is already. The furniture is already full, air breezes through the room, day is dry-eyed and disquiet. There is a welter. Salads float across the room. There should be maroons, more maroons where he said we should stand at the end across from the little beach. But frankly we get tired of living out options. The chase is too near though unseen, a superhighway densely screened by trees. What brought us here, you may ask. That and the wonder of having something to confess, "own up" to. You and he have had words on the subject countless times in the past, which more or less insures there's more to come. Say what? But the conscious arrow veers to the north; like a shriek it seizes its direction. If this is the way to go it must be the way forward, like you don't have to move except in it. I had seen him down by the laundry one day, caught him looking up here as though salvation were this place of drying. But we can't send him away, can we? Especially now that it's come dark over the turbaned foreheads, faces like dust-streaked slate. It's my fault. Still it's right that we are on this hill, falling, escaping the crowded paths and the sunset. *More's the pity*, he said. By what mystery are we compounded of loam and spindrift? Whose face is painted on the shield? What's going to happen when we all get a load of a little of what's going on, even though it's enough to hide the ghost armies' lateral advance, the slightly irregular tread comprised of many shuffling forms, tottering toward they know not what untidy denouement? It may happen then as it has in the past that the spider king will unhitch himself to plummet directly into our daily affairs as they seemed on the point of opening, creating themselves and us as a by-product? And we assume that mushroom-like cape, shroud of not knowing and begging for an unlikely handout? It's November, you see, the time that promises everything it has just sucked up through a straw. Primroses, adolescent love, glistering toy motorcycles, *airs d'opérette*—you name it, but not before I've managed my exit and found a seat in the stalls.

They never bother to check those things. I cooked a pot of nice peas. I took the A train up here again. I just don't think it's particularly calm up here. "The hills of home." Get up, get this thing done, get out alive.

Want me to fix it? Oh man I want to try to do something just as hard as you can. For as I told you I couldn't do it. Next time we sit around promise me you'll cry. Or all your breath will be spent on the wind from the city, your tears round as obelisks at an orgy. Don't cry, you can come. Pray with us here. Rejoice in the thousands of cousins that support you, and after that never say the dark cart isn't coming to get you. It is but it won't let you pass by. 'Twill be as father and mother and stepgrandchildren to you, mark these words. Never go over into the garden when the path is clearly marked. We must let you be quoted or their smirk would end the world. The salley gardens—what were they anyway? Something we were supposed to know about, or something we weren't and all hell would break loose? It's calm. Here we may sup. I have brought you your dinner, *contre vents et marées*, I have helped and been as a customer to you. Do not reject me this time, again.

Come right in and sit down. Can I offer you something? A glass of sparkling cider, perhaps? How it doesn't sparkle! It's a bit lonely here, which is mostly my fault. The windowpanes are tinted a faint violet, which causes a wistful light in the room that one isn't wholly aware of. I should have them replaced but they are old and very valuable. A few have been broken and replaced, and the resulting mismatched brightness here and there is unsettling. I'm the first and no doubt the last to admit it. Don't try talking to Doris and Dolores, there'd be no point. They're in a photograph, window shopping in Oxford Street, circa 1937 or 1936. They seem very smartly turned out, don't you agree— Dolores in her little leopard cape and matching toque; Doris in a dark pillbox hat in whose veil black pom poms are embedded. Soon they will enter a large movie palace near Leicester Square. The feature hasn't begun yet but there's a newsreel with Mussolini ranting about Ethiopia or something. Next is a serial starring the American actor Kane Richmond, a tall, dark, good-looking man who seems to prefer the company of horses and dogs to that of men as well as women. Maybe that's why his shyness seems about right. Dolores is already groping in her purse for a handkerchief. The villains have Kane trapped in a barn and are starting to set fire to it. Then it's all over, for this week at least. The feature is beginning and the music wells up very lively and somber; it's a romance starring that lovely Greta Gynt.

Pass me a mint, dear. I'm afraid my mascara is streaked. It must look awful in this rapid play of flashing lights and shadows. Heavens! It seems the projector is broken. We'll have to wait in the dark. Only they've turned the lights up now. Somebody is going to make some kind of announcement.

Or perhaps a nicely buttered roll would satisfy? A taste like chestnut flooded his head. Doorbell rang, sweet kitties sang. It was dark down in his pants when he crouched over to see where the taunting was coming from, while we kittens emoted on the floor. There is so much to oversee, always.

Sometimes it comes in the form of delayed correspondence. Those wilted irises you threw out had been sent, months ago, by an admirer, someone who knew your preferences, that you liked their limited color and fragrance. Now it's hopeless to find the accompanying note, unless you remember where you put it. Unlikelier than it seems, though not beyond the remotest likelihood. We shall oversee these, but there will be other, collateral descendants, ocean-broad, until you get the feeling again. Again, there is nothing remote about it.

Arguably,

the park light forecasts rangers, their oxides exit with the clamor of breeze. No one knows how many there are. Nobody has ever counted them. Which can seem strange given the iconic presence, but really not so much as having been given over to selectivity and passive anger.

What about you? More nuts and bolts to which you wish you was livin' up to? The strange side riders were there but no one knows when it could have been a century ago, he assented. Everybody's always been interested in meanders, hero and meander, so I think you need to stand up to door. Have some more rhubarb grunt. Where was I?

An Unspecified Amount

Someone must have been telling lies about John A. It happened this way: all day long he would sit on the front porch, watching people and cars go by, tugging on his briar pipe. Except for his meals, which he took at the kitchen table, he would remain on the porch from dawn until it got quite dark, summer and winter, except for periods of extreme cold. Even then he could survey the street through a species of panopticon he had rigged up, which he liked to say was better than television, since it was free and never required adjustment. He said this mostly to himself since he rarely spoke to others, having little occasion to do so. He was not one of those people who sit and wave at cars and passersby with a cheery greeting. The one exception to his code of silence was Rachel, his cleaning woman who came twice a week, and even then his speech concerned mainly practical household matters.

One day a Fuller Brush man happened by, and, undiscouraged by John's laconic replies to his attempts at small talk, seated himself in the wicker chair where John would sit to read the newspaper, and was the only piece of porch furniture except for a glider where he would recline and occasionally take a nap, though this rarely happened since it prevented him from observing the activity in the street. Finding that his observations concerning traffic and the weather were not rebuffed, though scarcely encouraged, the man proceeded to expand on other topics such as the decline of the neighborhood.

très modéré

This irritated and frustrated John, who had been expecting a sales pitch for the brushes, and had already begun preparing a reply to the effect that he was amply provided with cleaning utensils and employed a person whose duties included ascertaining that nothing was lacking in that department. He had begun casting about for other ways of ridding himself of this pest, when the latter suddenly startled him by drawing his attention to a large package which the postman had evidently left next to the front door, whose mail slot would have been too narrow to accommodate it.

"What do you suppose is in there?" the stranger asked, a bit impertinently it seemed to John.

"Oh, it's probably some boots I ordered from L.L. Bean," John answered shiftily, aware as he did so that the package obviously contained nothing of the sort and that he had just unwittingly opened new avenues in a conversation in a conversation that was fast becoming vexatious.

The salesman however let the matter rest there. Or was he considering the most effective way to irk John even further?

Fried Mackerel and Frozen Peas

If only for that, you see, she'd accepted to go only as far as the parking garage. Like a blanket like a metallic cast to the air that obscures its tint and original purpose, she was being dragged back to answer the questions in the questionnaire that seemed to require no answers, since the questions had already been asked in almost identical wording. Questions about the color of the eyes

and oh I think so
know too much about me—it
doesn't care—the others are old
and arise from their griefs
as from a deep sleep. I must
have had this dream someone's accepted
as part of me—I have only to dress
for it to be over now. The king sent his
heralds through out the land to try
and find me—in the end one of them did.
I refused to go with him. So the king himself
came to my cottage door
and rapped three times. Then
and only then did I let him in.
We had a nice long conversation
in which we touched on many things
including my future and college education.

If it could matter now it would matter only to the sleep that awaits me and to this old piece of carpet. How long have you been here, chum? I never

saw you before and it's as though you've always been here, a part of my life, and an important one at that. It's that you don't want to bore me

with your being, isn't it? That's nice of you, but I'm clearing out. College? That's a tricky one. Maybe I'll just stay

somewhere, some place, like. There's lots of new openings. And the air, the air is rife with possibilities. Just don't tell anybody I told you about it. That would be the end, friend, the end.

* * *

The point is to find an extra-sensual way to be without it.
In the sixteenth century this could have been accomplished without anybody's realizing
it. Dogs would have run off as the wind picked up.
So many people stuck in motion up ahead can't deliver it.   The iceman is there.

So what if muslin is the new medium.

Her brother Mary was standing there, a stone finch.

It was time to take a pee, to turn back. It was time to head for home.

Fig. 13. Some of Ashbery's source materials for *The Kane Richmond Project*. Ashbery collaged excerpts and quotations from the three children's novels, *Tom Swift and His Rocket Ship* (1954), *Tom Swift and His Repelatron Skyway* (1963), and *Danger on Vampire Trail* (1971), into the poem. Also pictured is Ashbery's copy of volume four of *Serial Pictorial* with Kane Richmond (as Spy Smasher) on the cover. Photo credit: Sandy Noble.

Fig. 14. Table of contents for images
in volume four of *Serial Pictorial*.

SERIAL PICTORIAL
NUMBER FOUR

SPY SMASHER (REPUBLIC 1942)

SCENES IN THIS VOLUME:

Front Cover: Kane Richmond
Inside Front Cover: Kane Richmond, Frank Corsaro and Georges Renavent
Page One: Kane Richmond, Georges Renavent and Frank Corsaro
Page Two: Ken Terrell and Kane Richmond
Page Three: Kane Richmond, The Mask and Frank Corsaro
Page Four: Tom London and Kane Richmond
Page Five: Kane Richmond, Tom London and George Lewis (far right)
Page Six: Players and Kane Richmond
Page Seven: Frank Corsaro, Player, Carleton Young and Kane Richmond
Page Eight: Hans Schumm and Kane Richmond
Page Nine: Kane Richmond in dual role
Page Ten: Kane Richmond, Marguerite Chapman and stand-in for Richmond
Page Eleven: Kane Richmond and Frank Corsaro
Page Twelve: Kane Richmond
Inside Back Cover: Marguerite Chapman, Kane Richmond and Sam Flint
Back Cover: Marguerite Chapman and Kane Richmond

Fig. 15. Image from *Spy Smasher*
in volume four of *Serial Pictorial*.

A NOTE ON THE TEXT

On the following pages, a stanza break occurs at the bottom of the page (not including pages on which the break is evident because of the regular stanzaic structure of the poem): 7, 15, 16, 18, 19, 25, 31, 32, 54, 72, 77, 102, 117, 119, 124, 125, 132, 133, 147, 158, 176.

DATES AND ENTRIES

Ashbery wrote primarily on a typewriter and had a habit of dating his original typescripts. In drafts of longer works, this dating seemed to be a method of keeping track of where he left off, as he was often traveling between his house in Hudson and his NYC apartment. He would bring his work with him between these two homes, and typescripts had a way of getting waylaid, misplaced, or misordered (as with *The Kane Richmond Project*, wherein Ashbery's dating practices helped pages be reordered after some of the pages went missing for many months). Later in his career, after the late '90s when Kermani began overseeing the organization of his manuscript materials, Ashbery and/or Kermani sometimes noted the location in which the poem or entry was written. They did not adhere to this process consistently, but it provides us with an interesting framework in which to consider Ashbery's routines surrounding writing. Sometimes, Ashbery even stopped writing in the middle of a paragraph, sentence, or line (indicated by his placement of the date there) and picked up a few days later. In a single typescript, dates can be both written in and typed. To preserve flow and ease of reading, these dates were not included with the poems, but are instead organized here. The entries list the date of composition, followed by the first and last lines of text composed on that date, the page numbers where that text can be found in this book, and, when necessary, an explanatory note.

The History of Photography

March 22, 1993: ▮, *"First takers, first makers."* ... *"It is all a—how do you say? / — A fancy."* (7–8)

March 23, 1993: ▮, *"How could I have had such a good idea?"* ... *"a fool in time."* (8–9)
Because of the ambiguity of the date's placement in the margin, it is possible

that Ashbery ended this entry earlier, with the line "in the mind of the feeling man, who then gets his share," and that the final two lines of this section were added on March 24.

March 24, 1993: **II**, *"Francis Frith released the pyramids."* ... *"'devolves to this vastness and would-be vastness.'"* (**9–10**); *"But it would have turned out differently anyway,"* ... *"luminous confections / that walk you home, prop you against the front steps, and tiptoe off."* (**10–12**); *"Be thankful for this. I saved you."* (**12**)

Three separate entries marked this day.

March 29, 1993: **II**, *"'As some rich woman, on a winter's morn,"* ... *"and we ... we / were all ashore. It made a difference, that time."* (**12–14**)

March 31, 1993: **III**, *"Not to put too fine a point on it, you did"* ... *"Give me my scallop-shell of quiet"* (**15–17**)

April 1, 1993: **III**, *"and I'll be moseying along. The hagiography of this moment / is supported by meager underpinnings."* ... *"The others, then—no, no, you missed the turnoff / into that driveway. The others must lead you now."* (**17–18**)

April 2, 1993: **IV**, *"Oh, the legions of seagoing fish!"* ... *"A last chance of sorts, / gayer than the other, more in a mood to celebrate / the mood. Planted on the leeward side."* (**18–20**)

April 6, 1993: **V**, *"Opening sky, wandering life, the movers."* ... *"And whatever conceit we had nourished / then is as a bible now: no / parent or looking-glass: the sacred irony."* (**20–24**); *"And when he was gone, / some passed it along,"* ... *"And say, does / Nova Scotia play a part in any of this?"* (**24–25**)

Two entries marked this day: the first labeled "AM" and the second "PM."

April 8, 1993: **V**, *"Nothing bumptious about that, is there?"* ... *"and no room / for sorrow or anything resembling it, friends of my complexity."* (**25–27**)

April 9, 1993: **V**, *"You can sort of tell / which is the elders, by their glassy features / and celluloid reliquaries."* ... *"then folded / and put away like a deck chair."* (**27–29**)

April 12, 1993: **V**, *"Then what of the ostentatiously unmeritorious end of this day,"* ... *"And we get up and walk away, cured / of our nap, of her lullaby, / to the end of the road."* (29-31)

April 13, 1993: **VI**, *"Get out just the things you know—"* ... *"Try the cherries, they're / very good this year."* (31-32)

April 14, 1993: **VI**, *"You'd better copy the inside better / lest it melt strictly she said,"* ... *"and those whose modest eccentricities could pass unnoticed / in most crowds, but not in this one."* (33-35)

Because of the placement of the date in the margin, it is unclear whether Ashbery ended this entry with the above, or with the following dropped line: "Everywhere you looked."

April 15, 1993: **VI**, *"Everywhere you looked / tousled recruits stammered eulogies to the four seasons,"* ... *"The nectar and food are fine. The sisters are fine and resolute."* (35-37)

The Art of Finger Dexterity

May 11, 2007 [NYC]: **1. Application of the Fingers with Quiet Hand** (47)

May 15, 2007 [NYC]: **2. The Passing of the Thumb** (48); **3. Clarity in Velocity** (49)

Written on the same page as "Application of the Fingers with Quiet Hand."

May 17, 2007 [NYC]: **4. Light Articulation in Half-Staccato** (50)

May 18, 2007 [NYC]:

Written on the same page as the May 17 entry; Ashbery also wrote and crossed out a longer draft of a poem titled "Evenness in Double Runs" (see Appendix B, entry for p. 51).

May 19, 2007 [NYC]: **5. Evenness in Double Runs** (51); **6. Clarity in Broken Chords** (52)

Written on the same page.

May 20, 2007 [NYC]: **7. Changing Fingers on the Same Key** (53)

Written on the same page as the above entries from May 19.

May 24, 2007 [Hudson]: **8. Light Articulation of the Left Hand** (54–55)

May 30, 2007 [Hudson]: **9. Delicacy in Skips and Staccatos** (56)

June 1, 2007 [Hudson]: **10. Exercise for Thirds [I]** (57)

Written on the same page as "Delicacy in Skips and Staccatos."

June 1, 2007 [Hudson]: **10. Exercise for Thirds [II]** (58)

June 4, 2007 [Hudson]: **11. Skill in Alternating Fingers** (59)

June 9, 2007 [NYC]: **12. Flexibility of the Left Hand** (60)

June 10, 2007 [NYC]: **13. Maximum Velocity** (61–62)

June 11, 2007 [NYC]: **14. Chord Passages** (63)

June 12, 2007 [NYC]: **15. Wide Position in Fortissimo** (64); **16. Alternating Fingers at Speed** (65)

Written on the same page.

June 15, 2007 [NYC]:

On this day, Ashbery composed an early draft of "Crossing the Hands Naturally and with a Fine Touch." The corresponding Czerny title for the seventeenth variation is actually "Minor Scales at High Speed," which he corrected for on the later draft of the poem. Ashbery crossed out the early draft with a large "X," indicating that he did not want it published (see Appendix B, entry for p. 66).

June 16, 2007 [NYC]: **17. Minor Scales at High Speed** (66)

Title changed from "Crossing the Hands Naturally and with a Fine Touch."

June 17, 2007 [NYC]: **18. Crossing the Hands Naturally and with a Fine Touch** (67)

June 18, 2007 [NYC]: **19. Tense Positions with a "Peaceful" Wrist** (68)

June 28, 2007 [Hudson]: **20. Double Octaves** (69); **21. Parallel Movement of the Hands [I]** (70–71)
   Written on the same page.

June 29, 2007 [Hudson]: **21. Parallel Movement of the Hands [II]** (72–73)

July 6, 2007 [Hudson]: **22. Exercise for the Trill** (74–75)

July 8, 2007 [Hudson]: **23. Light Touch of the Left Hand** (76)

July 9, 2007 [Hudson]: **24. The Thumb on the Black Keys with the Hand Absolutely Quiet** (77–78)

July 20, 2007 [NYC]: **25. Agility and Clarity** (79)

Late July, 2007 [Hudson]: **26. Maximum Velocity in Arpeggios** (80)

Sacred and Profane Dances

"Sacred and Profane Dances" is the only undated manuscript in this collection (see Appendix C).

21 Variations on My Room

August 21, 2002: **Sections 1–7**, *"The single best way to do it."* ... *"The pallor of Pallas / overcomes evening do's and don'ts."* (99–100)

August 24, 2002: **Sections 8–11**, *"In my dream I was in Paris,"* ... *"Father in his little house / took a bath. It was almost time for the news."* (100–101)

It appears that Ashbery wrote the eleventh, final line of section 11, "The trolley arrived in time for dinner," on the following day, August 25, since the typed date is aligned with the penultimate tenth line. Additionally, the left justification of the eleventh line is slightly out of line with the rest of its stanza.

August 25, 2002: **Sections 11–13**, *"The trolley arrived in time for dinner."* . . . *"So on my day off, I // took the long trek out of the city. My reward is solitude."* (101-3)

August 27, 2002: **Sections 13–15**, *"So get a life. It's been real. I mean really real."* . . . *"One has to endure / certain systems, then profit by them later in the crust of events."* (103-4)

September 3, 2002: **Section 16**, *"We reject these. Oh I am sure / it was as serious then to be struggling / as it is now."* . . . *"It comes as no surprise to learn that winter is on the way / with headlands and diamond aigrettes, and the lightness."* (104-5)

September 9, 2002: **Sections 17–18**, *"Still hungry? Read on."* . . . *"'I hope we get the rest of the day off, genius boy,' Bud said shyly."* (105-6)

The Kane Richmond Project

April 23, 2002: **Spy Smasher** (117-19); **Perils of Nyoka** (119); **The Devil Diamond** (119-20)

April 30, 2002: **The Lost City** (121-22)

May 1, 2002: **Racing Blood**, *"Of all the rotten excuses."* . . . *"That's what it's coming to, to true blue."* (122-24)

May 6, 2002: **Racing Blood**, *"'Dear' had life tinged on it? Not on my watch, / they don't."* . . . *"It was an end anyway. No hiding place."* (124-26)

May 7, 2002: **Racing Blood**, *"Now I had nine or ten pages of copy."* . . . *"A mixed bag, but so it is written.'"* (126-28)

May 8, 2002: **Racing Blood**, *"The church gives you a dime, don't complain."* ... *"We'll all hang around together for a while after that."* (128–29)

May 13, 2002: **Racing Blood**, *"God doesn't expect a perfect score / most of the time, but sometimes the idea occurs: / What am I doing this for?"* ... **A Hard Man**, *"Some other year, maybe, / out of the parade of them, each with its majorettes / and streamers, but not today. You've guessed it. He's passed out. Again."* (129–32)

Undated entry: **The President's Dream**, *"Tourists assemble beneath the vast diorama."* ... *"Curtain shuddered delicately and withdrew."* (132–33)

May 20, 2002: **[untitled] "Kane was a righteous dude, heat-packing."** ... *"Soon it would be time to break out the champagne again."* (133–35)

May 21, 2002: **[untitled] "Kane was a righteous dude, heat-packing."** *"Kane was lost in the Métro, / somewhere between Plaisance and Pernety."* ... *"And then said nothing more."* (135–36)

May 22, 2002: **Chapter Seven** (136–37)

May 29, 2002: **The Mist Rolls in from the Sea** (137–38)

June 1, 2002: **A Lost Dog**, [epigraph] ... *"'That caterwaulin' alone could scare the wits out o' any critter,' Rinty reflected."* (140)
    Ashbery began this entry with the epigraph. (See Appendix E, entry for p. 140 for details on the sequencing of this section.)

June 2, 2002: **A Lost Dog**, *"In the fullness of time a foolish man did a good thing."* ... *"It was weirdly painted in psychedelic colors."* (141)

June 3, 2002: **Dog Overboard!** (139)

Undated entry: **Dog and Pony Show** (139)

June 4, 2002: **My Own Best Customer**, *"Bronze building borders chafe at the cat's slow progress."* ... *"We will be BORED."* (141–42)

June 5, 2002: **My Own Best Customer**, *"If it's life, it's* real *life." ... "Some day I am going to write about that."* (142)

June 10, 2002: **My Own Best Customer**, *"If only what between me and you / never happened." ... "Unfortunately there is no one who can advise you on these things—no one whose advice you'd be willing to take, anyways. Me and Buster, we—"* (143–44)

June 13, 2002: **My Own Best Customer**, *"Life should be simple and fashionable."* ... *"No one here was going to remember any of this for very long."* (144–45)

June 17, 2002: **My Own Best Customer**, *"I thought it odd—but what do I know?"* ... *"They were postulated on the same plane, and adults had seen them. Rex was almost certain of that."* (145–46)

June 18, 2002: **My Own Best Customer**, *"But how to distinguish between sincerity and feigned sincerity." ...* **Dog of the Limberlost**, *"Nothing much comes to cheat us / of this vapor."* (146–48)

June 21, 2002: **Dog of the Limberlost**, *"Cheese—at the moment? Nutcases." ... "William Biggs died some years ago."* (148)

Undated entry: **Sex on the River** (148–49)

June 24, 2002: **A Long and Sleepy History**, [epigraphs] ... *"A few more moments and the wreath of cares is done."* (150–51)
    Ashbery began this entry with the epigraphs.

June 25, 2002: **A Long and Sleepy History**, *"Dena's mother was sound asleep." ... "'BARBARA?' The voice began like thunder, pulling itself up into a cloudlike shape, then expiring for what seemed like hours, with something like tact, though this was not the time for it."* (151–52)

June 26, 2002: **A Long and Sleepy History**, *"If only I had studied a little harder I might recognize the next chapter." ... "I bid you good night."* (152–53)

June 28, 2002: **A Long and Sleepy History**, *"Someday I swear I'm going to ... No, but what was he saying?" ... "We have brighter things to blind us. Now is never."* (153–54)

June 30, 2002: **A Long and Sleepy History**, *"It saves us for the sacredness of talk."* . . . *"Little wonder there are not many takers for the conclusiveness that erupts then."* (154)

July 1, 2002: **A Long and Sleepy History**, *"A listener told me not to 'worry' about perceived injustice." . . . "It must have been all the labor that went into it, but even more that it was useless, as faceless a feature of the landscape as existed then in those parts."* (154–55)

July 3, 2002: **A Long and Sleepy History**, *"Oh, I don't wonder. Does landscape really count?" . . . "This went on into the hereafter."* (155)

July 4, 2002: **A Long and Sleepy History**, *"Meanwhile, the attention of the Americans was caught by a herd of lyre-horned Ankole cattle grazing on the grassy slopes."* . . . **The Quitter**, *"Eventually I'll be issuing a public statement / but for now all I want to do is rest. And consider."* (155–56)

July 5, 2002: **The Quitter**, *"Sometimes it's enough just to believe in what could happen,"* . . . *"but the curving sandbar always suggests another time, a re-engagement."* (156–57)

July 9, 2002: **More about Drew** (157)

July 16, 2002: **Modern Sketch**, *"Sleep a weak hour"* . . . *"The fifth can't salute."* (158–59)

July 17, 2002: **Modern Sketch**, *"If so, why bother / sober ascending / Apple Annie"* . . . *"at every tip the lorded lark explodes / with the factory whistle in her darkling eyes. Drab pots."* (159–61)

July 20, 2002: **To Meet with My Father**, *"As I walked on amid fires, a young man approached." . . . "Bud looked up in amazement."* (161)

July 21, 2002: **To Meet with My Father**, *"The woman was just leaving. She had been overseas." . . . "After all it was much too late for that. Or so Uncle Possum opined."* (161–62)

August 13, 2002: **[untitled] "I liked the fourth declension—all those 'u's."** *... "You wouldn't want him to interrupt you."* (162)

August 14, 2002: **[untitled] "I liked the fourth declension—all those 'u's."** *"So the Emperor's clean clothes are brushed and folded and placed without undue reverence in the palissandre* crédence." *... "But the vast files haven't budged: like impassable moraines slowly absorbing the dark as the sky goes light, then fades behind them, creating a quizzical unbuilt architecture whose function only the absent ruler knows: like where the haha eases into the patient prairie beyond."* (162-63)

August 19, 2002: **Miss Otis Regrets Land's End**, *"We went to America, we didn't see what they were doing there." ... "There's no point in being younger about three guys. And now I believe you."* (163-64)

November 9, 2002: **[untitled] "Are you trying to stop us?"** *... "We can go back to being in the order of each other's beds, and the rugs beside them, and the chairs pushed against the bed to make a kind of steps leading to the floor—oh wasn't it like this last month and the one before that and the others stretching back into the coal dust of whatever it was doing before?"* (164-65)
See Appendix E about placement of this entry.

November 13, 2002: **[untitled] "Are you trying to stop us?"** *"It's only a matter of time before two handsome critics sink fingers of mush into whatever it is." ... "Then, though it was already late early evening, a young boy came around telling us all to go somewhere, somewhere not too far away but not a place we had heard of."* (165-66)

November 16, 2002: **[untitled] "Nothing if found convenient."** *... "All about us is ajar, like the door is or was the time you tried to break in, having lost your keys on some car seat."* (166)

November 18, 2002: **[untitled] "Nothing if found convenient."** *"They're everywhere in the trees, madam! There is another inside another for another time." ...* **There You Go!** *"What if they came by and saw us? What would people think?"* (166-70)

November 19, 2002: [untitled] "Why wait for another day to cross itself?" … "*Still it's right that we are on this hill, falling, escaping the crowded paths and the sunset.* More's the pity, *he said.*" (170)

November 24, 2002: [untitled] "Why wait for another day to cross itself?" "*By what mystery are we compounded of loam and spindrift?*" … "*Primroses, adolescent love, glistering toy motorcycles,* airs d'opérette—*you name it, but not before I've managed my exit and found a seat in the stalls.*" (170–71)

November 25, 2002: [untitled] "Why wait for another day to cross itself?" "*They never bother to check those things. I cooked a pot of nice peas.*" … "*Do not reject me this time, again.*" (171–72)

December 2, 2002: [untitled] "Why wait for another day to cross itself?" "*Come right in and sit down. Can I offer you something?*" … "*Somebody is going to make some kind of announcement.*" (172–73)

December 3, 2002: [untitled] "Why wait for another day to cross itself?" "*Or perhaps a nicely buttered roll would satisfy?*" … "*Again, there is nothing remote about it.*" (173)

December 4, 2002: "**Arguably,** *the park light forecasts rangers, their oxides exit with the clamor of breeze.*" … **An Unspecified Amount**, "*Someone must have been telling lies about John A. It happened this way: all day long he would sit on the front porch, watching people and cars go by, tugging on his briar pipe.*" (173–74)

"An Unspecified Amount" and "*très modéré*" were handwritten on two undated sheets of yellow legal pad paper before they were typed in these three entries (see Appendix E, entry for p. 174).

December 7, 2002: **An Unspecified Amount**, "*Except for his meals, which he took at the kitchen table, he would remain on the porch from dawn until it got quite dark, summer and winter, except for periods of extreme cold.*" … "*Finding that his observations concerning traffic and the weather were not rebuffed, though scarcely encouraged, the man proceeded to expand on other topics such as the decline of the neighborhood.*" (174–75)

December 10, 2002: **_très modéré_**, *"This irritated and frustrated John, who had been expecting a sales pitch for the brushes, and had already begun preparing a reply to the effect that he was amply provided with cleaning utensils and employed a person whose duties included ascertaining that nothing was lacking in that department."* ... **Fried Mackerel and Frozen Peas**, *"That would be the end, friend, the end."* (175–77)

December 11, 2002: **[untitled] "The point is to find an extra-sensual way to be without it."** ... *"It was time to take a pee, to turn back. It was time to head for home."* (177)

APPENDIX A: THE HISTORY

OF PHOTOGRAPHY

Composed March 22–April 15, 1993, this fifteen-manuscript-page poem was found May 2019 (in both stapled and unstapled photocopy versions) in a box in the basement of Ashbery and Kermani's Hudson home. No original typescript has been located. The unstapled photocopy includes changes that were not present in the stapled photocopy, and so the unstapled version, presumed to be more recent, appears in this collection. The poem was stored in a manila folder marked "Manuscripts—to be sorted by book, if there is one" (crossed out above was "Tuesday Evening[1]/ Rough Draft"), which contained a note inside reading "Miscellaneous Drafts, mostly '97, to be refiled." Whereas the other contents of this folder were shorter poems and fragments, it also contained very early, out-of-order drafts and printouts of *Girls on the Run* (1999). In the same box were drafts of other unfinished and unpublished works, along with original drafts of poems that later made their way into books and other publications.

While it is unclear whether Ashbery in his title is directly referring to Walter Benjamin's essay "A Short History of Photography" (1931), their projects are similar, if not linked. Readers familiar with Benjamin's work will know this essay as a reckoning with photography's complicated relationship to art, as well as one of the first texts in which Benjamin articulates his concept of "aura." The quality that images and objects experienced in person and in real time inherently possess, aura is "a peculiar web of space and time: the unique manifestation of a distance, however near it may be."[2] This "distance" stretches through Ashbery's poem, as both a feeling and a vantage point:

---

1. Ashbery's long poem "Tuesday Evening" appears in *Can You Hear, Bird: Poems*. Farrar, Straus and Giroux, 1995.

2. Walter Benjamin, "A Short History of Photography," *Screen* 13, no. 1 (Spring 1972): 20.

Never made a dime at this swamp
and some liken it to haze, as distance is draped
in the mind of the feeling man, who then gets his share
of surmise and stumbles off to bed,
a fool in time.[3]

The first images of Benjamin and Ashbery's works are strikingly occluded. Benjamin begins:

The fog surrounding the origins of photography is not quite as thick as that enveloping the beginnings of printing. In the case of the former it was perhaps more obvious that the hour of invention had arrived, for it had been apprehended by a number of people: men striving independently toward the same goal, that is, to capture images in the *camera obscura* which had certainly been known since Leonardo's time, if not before.[4]

Ashbery's playful opening presents a similar atmospheric occlusion, a sky "diapered" by clouds:

First takers, first makers.
The first sip of intelligence
splits the diapered sky, already crackled
with the losses that events are.[5]

"The History of Photography" contains references to both early and contemporary photographers and advancements in the technologies and modes of early photography. These "first takers," or the "makers" of early photography, clear a visual path in the sky. If events are "losses" that project their traces onto the sky, the photograph captures such events and refutes their existence as purely ephemeral.

Or, compare side by side these two passages, which both refer to the visiting

---

3. *Parallel Movement of the Hands*, 9.

4. Benjamin, 5.

5. *Parallel Movement of the Hands*, 7.

card and its role in the history of early photography, as well as the photographic image's link to capitalism and industry:

> Industry conquered the field with the visiting-card snapshot, its first manufacturer characteristically becoming a millionaire. It would not be surprising if the photographic practices which today, for the first time, direct our gaze back to that pre-industrial prime, turned out to be linked subterraneously with the crisis of capitalism.[6]

> Get out just the things you know—
> on the road excellent sunflowers, the ubiquitous *carte de visite*,
> demographics in which many a man's face is lost
> on Pennsylvania coal-mining towns, coming clear at the end.
> Wipe the slate clean, a name will be streaming there still.[7]

Ashbery wrote "The History of Photography" in 1993, the year following the publication of *Hotel Lautréamont* (1992), which contains several longer poems in numbered sections. Around the time "The History of Photography" was written, Ashbery would have been composing the poems in *And the Stars Were Shining* (1994), a book in which the individual poems rarely exceed two pages, save for the long title poem that ends the collection. "And the Stars Were Shining," first published in fall 1993 in *Conjunctions* magazine, bears structural resemblance to "The History of Photography." It makes sense, then, that Ashbery may have chosen to omit "The History of Photography" from his 1994 collection so as not to detract attention from its final, serial poem.

As is the case with drafts for many of Ashbery's longer works, the entries of "The History of Photography" are scrupulously dated. This dating shows an almost daily returning to the text, a period of dedicated attention. On April 15, 1993, Ashbery wrote "END" at the bottom of the fifteenth typescript page, making this one of the only works in the collection whose "unfinishedness" presents itself in the possibility that a "clean copy" was never prepared for publication.

---

6. Benjamin, 5.

7. *Parallel Movement of the Hands*, 31.

Section I (7)

7: *"splits the diapered sky, already crackled"*

This "splits" might easily have been "splats." It is unclear in this photocopy whether the "i" was transposed over the "a" in Ashbery's correction (he originally wrote and crossed out "expands"). "Splits" was chosen for its sonic association with "sip," its closeness to the original word, the slightly more pronounced boldness of the cursive "i," and because it carries the image of parting clouds. The word "crackled" here is a correction of an earlier "erzed," perhaps suggesting a material ribboned through with ore.[8]

7: *"The first person to be photographed was a man / having his boots cleaned. There were others / in the same street, but they moved and became / invisible. How calm I am!"*

A reference to inventor and early photographer Louis-Jacques-Mandé Daguerre's photograph of the Boulevard du Temple in Paris (1838–9), in which, because of the long exposure time, only the subjects who remained stationary, a boot shiner and his customer, were captured in the image. Although the street at that hour was bustling, the people in motion during the exposure did not appear in the daguerreotype.

7: *"Baron de Meyer saw the horse and it too moved on. / Nor was the lesson of satin lost on him."*

A clever collision of Baron Adolph de Meyer, the early twentieth-century portrait and fashion photographer, and Eadweard Muybridge's photographic study entitled *The Horse in Motion* (1878). Meyer titled a 1927 photograph of a woman *Nile Green Satin for Summer*.

8: *"Then too, as much escapes me as a tailor's dummy / in a photograph by Atget, taking in everything and nothing, / which caused the rain to fall one day."*

---

8. See fig. 1.

In 1925, French photographer Eugène Atget took a series of photos of mannequins in storefront windows on the Avenue des Gobelins in Paris. Atget's photographs would later prove important to the surrealists. Of the photographer and his vacated spaces, Benjamin observes,

> Atget was an actor who, repelled by his profession, tore off his mask and then sought to strip reality of its camouflage.... Indeed, Atget's Paris photos are the forerunners of surrealist photography; vanguard of the only really broad column which surrealism was able to set in motion. He was the first to disinfect the stuffy atmosphere spread by the conventional portrait photography of the period of decline. He cleansed this atmosphere, indeed cleared it altogether. He initiated the liberation of the object from the aura, which is the most incontestable achievement of the recent school of photography.... The city in these pictures is empty in the manner of a flat which has not yet found a new occupant. They are the achievements of surrealist photography which presages a salutary estrangement between man and his environment, thus clearing the ground for the politically-trained eye before which all intimacies serve the illumination of detail.[9]

Ashbery alludes to Atget's dummy photographs in another poem, published in slight variation in two collections, first in *And the Stars Were Shining* (1994) as "Sicilian Bird," and later as "Andante Misterioso" in *Can You Hear, Bird* (1995). He writes, "And wherever man sets his giant foot / petals spring up, and artificial torsos, / dressmakers' dummies. And an ancient photograph / and an ancient phonograph that carols // in mist."[10] It is likely that Ashbery wrote "Sicilian Bird" and "The History of Photography" during the same period, which may explain the crisscrossing references.

---

9. Benjamin, 20–21.

10. Ashbery, *Can You Hear, Bird*, 10.

9: *"Francis Frith released the pyramids. / Nègre produced the ogival mysteries, / Mapplethorpe the dissenting penis"*

Beginning with Francis Frith, Ashbery constructs a chain of influential photographers. Frith indeed "released" the pyramids and other Egyptian monuments via photographs, made using the early albumen method of photographic printing, on a series of very productive voyages beginning in 1856.[11] The first images many Europeans had ever seen of these structures, these photographs enabled Frith to start a successful postcard business in England selling images captured during his travels to Africa and the Middle East.[12]

Ashbery imagines the viewers of these early photographs in his introduction to an exhibition catalogue of photographer Lynn Davis's works:

> When the first traveler-photographers of the nineteenth century began bringing back and displaying their finds in the capitals of Europe and America, audiences must have found these artifacts doubly puzzling. First there were the subjects themselves: the Pyramids, Yosemite, the Taj Mahal, the Dead Sea, as few had ever seen them, in all their awkward, unapologetic grandeur. But perhaps even more surprising was the fact of photography itself. This new, ill-understood medium for capturing the "wonders of the world" was itself one. In a few short decades, of course, every family would have its Kodak, and snapshots of the Sphinx with Aunt Clara in the foreground would be a feature of many a parlor. The novelty of photography quickly became a commonplace.
>
> Lynn Davis's images take us back to the dawn of epic photography, when the shock of seeing remote sites hitherto only imagined was compounded by

---

11. Lisa Hostetler, "Biography: Francis Frith" The International Center of Photography, www.icp.org/browse/archive/constituents/francis-frith?all/all/all/all/0.

12. Ibid.

the astounding technical means that brought them into view, so that the dew or pollen of earliness still stippled their surfaces.[13]

After Frith comes Charles Nègre, a nineteenth-century French photographer known for his photographs of architecture. Ashbery is likely referring here to Nègre's images of French cathedrals (including Notre Dame in Paris). The final link is Robert Mapplethorpe, whose posthumous book of flower photographs, *Pistils* (1996), features an introduction by Ashbery: "The malign brilliance of his erotic pictures is present throughout, and nowhere more than in the portraits of flowers, impassive but somehow conspiring in their own corruptibility."[14]

10: "'*Grace under pressure is the only reasonable account / it can give of itself. But whence comes / this pressure?*'"

"Grace under pressure" is Ernest Hemingway's often-quoted definition of either "courage" or "guts," depending on the source.

12: "'As some rich woman, on a winter's morn, / Eyes through her silken curtains the poor drudge / Who with numb blacken'd fingers makes her fire— / At cockcrow, on a starlit winter's morn, When the frost flowers the whiten'd window panes— / And wonders how she lives, and what the thoughts / Of that poor drudge may be . . .'"

Ashbery noted in the margin that this quotation comes from Matthew Arnold's long narrative poem *Sohrab and Rustum* (1853), and that his edition of this work was a publication selected and introduced by Clifford Dyment: "'Sohrab + Rustum.' Dyment, p. 109."[15] The quotation that begins the last stanza of section II, "*like some young cypress, tall, and dark, and straight, / Which in a queen's*

---

13. John Ashbery, "Introduction to an Exhibition Catalogue: Lynn Davis," *Selected Prose*, ed. Eugene Richie. University of Michigan Press, 2004, 276–77.

14. Ashbery, "Introduction to Robert Mapplethorpe's *Pistils*," *Selected Prose*, 256.

15. See fig. 2.

secluded garden throws / Its slight dark shadow on the moonlit turf," is from the same source, as indicated by the notation "ibid" in the margin beside it; both quotations are from the same stanza in Arnold's poem.

Just a few years later, Ashbery quotes Arnold's poetry in a different poem. In "The Dong with the Luminous Nose" from *Wakefulness* (1998), Ashbery uses a line from "The Scholar-Gipsy": "Come, Shepherd, and again renew the quest," as the seventh line of his cento, sandwiching it between two quotes from Shakespeare.

13: "*Monotonously rings the little bell. / Eakins, skunked by depression, opted for cheese rinds, / a lorry driver's running balls—these are things / that cannot be painted—polevaulting figures, Muybridge's hopping woman— / because one vignette sheds another, cancels its own credibility / in a fever of slight adjustments, ends up a mass, twisted.*"

This passage refers to American painter, photographer, and sculptor Thomas Eakins. Initially inspired by Muybridge's studies of motion, Eakins produced his own photographic studies of human and equine movement using methods he deemed more scientifically accurate, including a series featuring a pole vaulter.[16] Both Eakins and Muybridge captured images of figures hopping and jumping. Eakins's interest in photography stemmed from a desire to paint figures with greater precision.

14: "'like some young cypress, tall, and dark, and straight, / Which in a queen's secluded garden throws / Its slight dark shadow on the moonlit turf,'"

See entry for p. **12**, "*As some rich woman, on a winter's morn . . .*"

Section III (15)

15: "'*the black or dark purple sclerotium of the genus* Clavicept / *that occurs as a clubshaped body which replaces the seed / of various grasses (as rye)*' *into a 'soft horny stub*

---

16. Lloyd Goodrich, *Thomas Eakins: His Life and Work*. Whitney Museum of Art, 1933, 65–71.

/ about the size of chestnut occurring as a normal / growth in the tufts of hair on the back of the fetlock / in the horse'?"

These variant definitions of "ergot" might appear next to one another in an encyclopedia or dictionary entry. The source of these definitions appears to be Ashbery's favorite dictionary (*Webster's New International*, 2nd ed., unabridged, 1941), which sat by his desk in Hudson.[17]

17: *"Give me my scallop-shell of quiet / and I'll be moseying along."*

In *Can You Hear, Bird* (1995), Ashbery begins his poem "Safe Conduct" with "The coast is clear. Bring me my scallop shell of quiet, / my spear of burning gold."[18] In his notes to the second Library of America volume of Ashbery's poetry, Mark Ford observes that "Give me my scallop shell of quiet" is taken "[f]rom the first line of the anonymous poem 'The Passionate Man's Pilgrimage' (1604), often ascribed to Sir Walter Raleigh."[19]

Section V (20)

20: "un peu, beaucoup, / passionnément,"

A fragment of the French version of the game in which one plucks petals from a flower in hopes of divining romantic prospects; English speakers may recognize the game as "He loves me / he loves me not." In French, the game isn't so black and white, offering several possibilities: the complete phrase is *"Il m'aime un peu, beaucoup, passionnément, à la folie, pas du tout,"* "He loves me a little, a lot, passionately, madly, not at all."

21: *"Winter was like this, / preventing furring,"*

---

17. David Kermani, email to ES, Apr. 29, 2020.

18. John Ashbery, "Safe Conduct," *Can You Hear, Bird*, in *Collected Poems, 1991–2000*, ed. Mark Ford. Library of America, 2017, 481.

19. Ibid., 801.

In the photocopied typescript, this line reads "Winter [X] was like this, / pre-vent[illegible] furring." The uppercase typewritten "X" between "Winter" and "was" covers either a lowercase "t" or "i." Ashbery was perhaps about to write "Winter is" and then decided to change the tense. The "s" of "prevents" is covered by an illegible written symbol that seems to combine elements of a "t" and a "g." I chose "preventing" over "prevents" or "prevented" to agree with the tense of the statement and approximate the written correction.

24: *"(An Egyptian dog, the only living being known to have been killed by a meteorite—/ thanks, Robert E. Ripley)"*

A reference to the Nakhla meteorite, which fell to Earth from Mars on June 28, 1911. The meteorite landed in Egypt, and the story goes that a fragment of the object broke off and killed a dog on impact, reducing it to dust. It is unclear whether this tall tale was ever included in a *Ripley's Believe It or Not!* encyclopedia or comic strip. Cartoonist and curio-collector Robert Ripley's middle initial, incidentally, is not "E" but "L" (for his first name, LeRoy).

25: *"(for love has fled; maybe, maybe though, it was always empty, / its little door ajar, its cuttlebone holder not unhinged, still / viable. No, love at last left us; no use / debating whether it exited, for it is gone. / Fomenting crises was its thing. And it is happy / and sad now, tears streaming down that smiling face / like rain streaking sunshine.* I know nothing / of that, but someone left an envelope for you."

Ashbery neglected to close this parenthetical. He originally added a closed parenthesis after "for it is gone," but crossed it out with a typed uppercase "X" and continued on. Rather than guess where the mark should go, I have chosen to leave it open, allowing the reader to decide where this particular aside might end.

27: *"And behold, three trancelike / sisters accosted me on the steep path"*

These three sisters, with their attachments to "grief and destiny," who transform into "three solemn sisters / in sunbonnets"[20] and recur again in the last line

---

20. *Parallel Movement of the Hands*, 34.

of the poem, are likely a reference to the three witches or "weird sisters" from Shakespeare's *Macbeth*.

28–29: *"First, the animated equestrian film: / it's true, all its feet are off the ground / simultaneously, its fetlocks / and withers waving triumphally in air, the end / of gravity, that insulating dominance. / There was no rider in that instance, but later / one is glimpsed in the background, then / in the foreground, a jockey of moonbeams, soon / to occupy center stage in the struggle for aesthetic significance"*

A reference to *The Horse in Motion* (1878), Muybridge's sequences of photographs that reveal the movements of a horse at different gaits. By capturing the gallop as a series of frames, Muybridge showed that there is a single point at which all of the horse's hooves leave the ground, something the human eye was not before able to discern unaided. As Ashbery notes, there is no rider in some of the series, while others have a rider or a driver. Later, Muybridge animated these still photographs using a zoopraxiscope, a precursor to the film projector. Such innovations earned him the epithet "the godfather of cinema."

Section *VI* (31)

36: *"Easy learner, easy burner. / The first photographers / who got it right knew what they were doing."*

These lines echo the first lines of the poem, "First takers, first makers. / The first sip of intelligence / splits,"[21] launching us into a final, concise treatment of the history of photography and Ashbery's witty diagnosis of the progression, innovations, and generations of artists who make up the "history" of any form.

---

21. Ibid., 7.

APPENDIX B: THE ART

OF FINGER DEXTERITY

This manuscript, written between mid-May and late July 2007 in both Hudson and NYC, was kept in the same file drawer in NYC as *The Kane Richmond Project*. There were two folders, one for the original typescript and one containing a set of photocopies. Ashbery heavily and carefully line edited the original typescripts, but made no additional changes to the photocopies.

In a 2007 profile by Nina Shengold, Ashbery mentioned composer Carl Czerny directly, though did not say that he had recently been working on a series of poems based on *The Art of Finger Dexterity*: "Lately, I've been listening with a lot of interest to 'The Art of Finger Dexterity' by Czerny, which was written to torture piano students. . . . It's mostly silly little tunes ornamented in a very complicated way to stretch the fingers to the limits of endurance. It's kind of beautiful because of having been written from that angle, to educate the fingers."[1]

Kunst der Fingerfertigkeit, or *The Art of Finger Dexterity* (Op. 740), was, indeed, an instructional composition. Czerny's numerous pedagogical compositions tend to eclipse the other music written by Beethoven's most notable pupil and Franz Liszt's teacher.[2] Ashbery owned several versions of the piece of music: two copies of the same cassette tape in NYC, and one CD (a different recording)

---

1. Nina Shengold, "Perennial Voyager: John Ashbery at Home," *Chronogram* [Hudson Valley Edition] (Sep. 2007): 57.

2. "Czerny was a great musician and prolific composer whose fate it was to be remembered only for his exercises." For a brief overview of Czerny's contributions to the history of classical music composition and performance, I recommend Leon Botstein's program note to *Beethoven's Pupil*, a concert performed at the Avery Fisher Hall at Lincoln Center on Nov. 14, 2004, www.leonbotstein.com/blog/beethovens-pupil.

in Hudson.[3] Based on the dimensions of the photocopied liner notes kept with the typescript and used for reference, and the fact that by 2007 Ashbery was listening to music on a CD player, it is likely they came from the CD in Hudson.

When I asked Kermani whether or not Ashbery was listening to the corresponding Czerny pieces *while* he wrote the poems, he said it was safe to assume that Ashbery listened "at least some of the time" as he was writing.[4] Intermittently, Kermani documented the classical music Ashbery often listened to as he wrote, noting the piece of music and date on lists that he kept in folders with the dated poem typescripts. Readers and scholars interested in seeing these lists can eventually find them at Harvard's Houghton Library. One of the most interesting duties of my job as Ashbery's assistant was ordering the often obscure recordings that he would circle in issues of *American Record Guide* and *Fanfare*, classical music review magazines to which he subscribed.

It is unclear whether Ashbery designated a title for this specific project. There is no indication of a title on any of the photocopies or original typescripts themselves. On the folder containing photocopies of the poems, "Czerny Variations" is written in my own handwriting on the tab. I only vaguely remember labeling this folder, but am unable to recall whether *Czerny Variations* was Ashbery's title. It is more likely that I quickly labeled the folder so it could be located later on. Some of these poems were published under the title *Czerny Variations* in issue 225 of *The Paris Review*. After this publication, I was able to locate a chronological list of Ashbery's poems from 2007, in which the project is called *The Art of Finger Dexterity*, as well as, simply, *Czerny*, indicating that Ashbery may have had two separate titles in mind. The entry reads "Art of Finger Dexterity, The (24 of anticipated 50 sections, 5/15 – 7/9/07, NYC and Hudson; short title:

---

3. In NYC: Carl Czerny and Vivien Harvey Slate, *The Art of Finger Dexterity: Op. 740*. New York: Musical Heritage Society, 1976, cassette tape. In Hudson: Carl Czerny and Francesco Libetta, *The Art of Finger Dexterity: Op. 740*. Pleasantville, NY: VAI Audio, 2006, compact disk.

4. David Kermani, conversation with ES, Feb. 16, 2020.

Czerny – see separate list)." The last poem included on this list, "Pale Im-promptu," is dated December 16, 2007. The note above suggests that whatever it was going to be titled, Ashbery still considered this project "active" or "in-progress" in December 2007, almost five months after he wrote the last poem in the series. The "separate list" mentioned omits poems 25 and 26 and calls the project *The Art of Finger Dexterity*.

I have used the longer title because it aligns with the concept of the project, as Ashbery named each poem after the first twenty-six of the fifty variations. Wanting to honor the suggestion of an alternate title containing Czerny's name, I took a cue from Ashbery's *Girls on the Run* (1999), in which "after Henry Darger" appears underneath the title on the poem's first page.

In the folder, the poems were organized in descending numerical order, which seemed to me not intentional but merely the way the pages were stacked as Ashbery finished poems. For the purposes of this book, I have arranged them in ascending order. In many cases, he composed more than one short poem on a single page, but here I have given each poem its own page. In instances where Ashbery left poems untitled and only included the number of the variation, I have supplied the corresponding Czerny title, and where Ashbery has omitted the number, I have inserted it as well. Where there is a discrepancy between Ashbery's and Czerny's titles, I've attempted to determine what is intentional and what is merely a transcription error.

1. Application of the Fingers with Quiet Hand (47)

In the Czerny liner notes, this title is "Articulation of the Fingers with Quiet Hand." This is the only instance in this manuscript where a different word is supplied, though sometimes Ashbery's titles do vary from those of his source material. I kept Ashbery's variation, which contains its own, slightly spooky magic.

5. *Evenness in Double Runs* (51)

Ashbery originally used this title for a twenty-eight-line, three-stanza poem, written the day before this one-line poem. The longer poem, composed on the same page as "LightSkill Articulation in Half-Staccato," was cut after extensive edits. Ashbery indicated the omission of the earlier version with his typical bold diagonal slash through the text.

The line "O happy something" does not appear in this earlier version. Lines, words, and phrases from this omitted poem, including the last line, "Did ~~that~~ [this] ever happen?" recur, with modification, in "Clarity in Broken Chords."

6. *Clarity in Broken Chords* (52)

See entry above.

52: *"and through the* tonnelle*'s damp falls / as though this were a hirsute day / on the river"*

In the original typescript, Ashbery wrote "tonnelles." It is unclear whether he meant for this word to be possessive plural or possessive singular. The singular was chosen for simplicity.

9. *Delicacy in Skips and Staccatos* (56)

Ashbery tucked this short poem into "Zymurgy," the final poem in his 2009 collection *Planisphere*. It is quite possible he was consulting an old handwritten fragment and not the Czerny manuscript itself. "Zymurgy" also includes the final line from "Exercise for Thirds [I]": "No but I'd like to talk to you about it."[5]

---

5. *Parallel Movement of the Hands*, 57.

10. Exercise for Thirds (57–58)

There are two poems numbered "10" and titled "Exercise for Thirds." This doubling occurs again later with "Parallel Movement of the Hands."

11. Skill in Alternating Fingers (59)

Fragments in this poem also appear in "Double Whoopee," published in Ashbery's 2012 collection *Quick Question*. Additionally, "Double Whoopee" includes the line "Worrier. You understand?" in "Exercise for Thirds [II]."[6]

13. Maximum Velocity (61)

61–62: "*Please be this visitor who sees, / not the one who tended / a vitamin shop on the edges, / rolling or coming around.*"

Ashbery originally typed "Please be the visitor who sees," and penciled "this?" above the "the."

14. Chord Passages (63)

63: "*tire / irons forged against a bettered time, / period of grace for the branded ones.*"

Ashbery struck through the "the," so that the last line would have read "period of grace for branded ones." However, he also penciled "the?" below, questioning this deletion. Here I have followed what seems to be his second thought.

---

6. Ibid., 58.

15. *Wide Position in Fortissimo* (64)

64: *"Indications of sonatine continue to haunt the white / ogre careless of the Thuille-influenced backlit / diorama"*

Ludwig Thuille (1861–1907) was an Austrian composer.

17. *Minor Scales at High Speed* (66)

Ashbery may have lost his place in the liner notes, at first titling poem 17 "Crossing the Hands Naturally and with a Fine Touch" in both an early version that was cut and the version here, which he later corrected in pencil to "Minor Scales at High Speed." The early version, not included here, is forty-one lines (two sextets followed by a stanza of twenty-nine lines). I have found no subsequent poems that reuse any of the language in this omitted draft, through which Ashbery drew a large "X."

19. *Tense Positions with a "Peaceful" Wrist* (68)

In the liner notes, quotation marks surround "peaceful wrist." I have left Ashbery's title as it is here, with "peaceful" emphasized only.

68: *"only that all points are equidistant and pleased, / and part of summer, the part of you that got on with it."*

The initial lines were "only that all points are equidistant and pleased, / swimmer, sympathizer—the part of you that got on with it." Ashbery also tried a variation of "swimmer, sympathizer" earlier in the poem, but crossed it out, while making many other substitutions, two of which return to the language of the title:

~~But~~ If not, let us hide our toes,

    fall backward into stagnant ether that is what

    rises ~~to meet us~~ at the end of all days, of all voyages

    in and from the parlor. ~~So, my little sea urchin, swimmer,~~

    ~~sympathizer,~~ We must ~~convert~~ [translate] what is ~~meticulous~~ [tense]

    into ~~rigorous~~ [peaceful] outcomes that will ripple back

    to foreign origins, not ~~seeming~~ [wishing] to know the name

In the final line, "swimmer, sympathizer" is crossed out, and the correction "and part of summer, ~~swimmer, sympathizer~~" is written underneath. In total, he crossed this phrase out three times in one page.[7] After consulting with Rosanne Wasserman, who also knew Ashbery's handwriting, the word "summer," which was once indecipherable to me, revealed itself. Ashbery's final omission of the phrase allows for the beautiful parallelism of the last line, "And part of summer, the part of you that got on with it."

20. *Double Octaves* (69)

69: *"Did you get a hat today?"*
    This is also the beginning line of "Exercise for Thirds [II]."

21. *Parallel Movement of the Hands* (70-73)

This title is used for two consecutive poems, as with "Exercise for Thirds."[8]

73: *"The wind blows where it wants. / The wind will carry it away."*
    These lines (in slight variation) also end Ashbery's poem "Saps at Sea," from his 2012 collection *Quick Question*.

---

7. See fig. 3.
8. See figs. 4 and 5.

APPENDIX C: SACRED
AND PROFANE DANCES

The three prose poems in this section are the only undated works in this collection. Two drafts of the first piece, "ATTAINDER," were typed on cheap newsprint, whereas "Sacred and Profane Dances" was typed on the high-quality, thick, Eaton cotton-fiber paper more typical of Ashbery's original typescripts. In his later career, Ashbery typed his poems almost exclusively on Crane paper, only sold in specialty stationery stores. Before his loyalty to Crane became habitual, he would have bought Eaton, which was more widely available.[1] There are other clues that point to these poems being from an earlier period, the most compelling of which is the capitalization of "ATTAINDER."[2] Ashbery capitalized his titles until around 1952, after which he began to phase out this practice. After 1955, it is rare to find a poem with a capitalized title.[3]

David Kermani found these typescripts in Ashbery's NYC study in a tall white bookcase that contained important correspondence, translations, and professional papers, but little original manuscript material. Grouped together were "ATTAINDER" (four pages, two drafts) and "Sacred and Profane Dances" (three pages, one draft), typed on the same typewriter, along with four pages of computer typescripts incorporating Ashbery's handwritten revisions for "ATTAINDER" and "Tempest," all fastened together with a paper clip. The typeface of the original typescripts of the first two sections was unfamiliar to me, which further suggested it was older than the other works in this book. The original

---

1. David Kermani, conversation with ES, Feb. 16, 2020.

2. See fig. 6.

3. Karin Roffman, email to ES, May 4, 2020.

typescript pages for "Tempest," the third prose piece, were not found with this grouping and have yet to be located.

While it's unlikely that "Tempest" was part of the same project as "AT-TAINDER" and "Sacred and Profane Dances," since it breaks from the narrative exploration of the Parable of the Ten Virgins, it is plausible that it is part of the same period of prose experimentation, and was found (as a computer typescript) with the other works. I hesitated about whether to include it, but ultimately decided that its charms as a text outweighed its status as an outsider. Since the series as a whole was untitled, I have named it after its central poem.

Eugene Richie, Ashbery's former assistant, editor of his *Selected Prose* (2004), and coeditor (with Rosanne Wasserman) of his *Collected French Translations* (Prose and Poetry, 2014), remembers making the facsimile computer typescripts of "AT-TAINDER" and "Tempest," from the original typescript drafts for possible inclusion in *Selected Prose* in the late 1990s.[4] It is unclear why he did not type "Sacred and Profane Dances," obviously part of the same series, though perhaps it was written later. According to Richie, Ashbery ultimately felt that these prose poems didn't fit with the nonfiction work of that collection, and so they were not included.[5] Ashbery's short story from 1952, "The Egyptian Helen," was also left out of the collection for this reason.[6] For more information regarding the selection process for *Selected Prose*, please refer to Richie's introduction to that collection.

The first two pieces, "ATTAINDER" and "Sacred and Profane Dances," loosely follow the events of the Parable of the Ten Virgins, attributed to Jesus, as relayed in the Gospel of Matthew. This story is meant to symbolize the Second Coming of Christ, who in this tale is presented as a bridegroom and the virgins as bridesmaids. When the bridegroom arrives unexpectedly, the "wise" virgins who have oil in their lamps are welcomed to the wedding feast, and the "foolish" virgins who aren't ready for the festivities are punished and cast out:

---

4. Eugene Richie, conversation with ES, Jan. 17, 2020.

5. Ibid.

6. First published in Rosanne Wasserman, "Helen of Troy: Her Myth in Modern Poetry" (PhD diss., CUNY 1986). Reprinted in *Gnosis*, 11 (Winter 1995).

Then the Kingdom of Heaven will be like ten virgins who took their lamps and went out to meet the bridegroom. Five of them were foolish, and five were wise. Those who were foolish, when they took their lamps, took no oil with them, but the wise took oil in their vessels with their lamps. Now while the bridegroom delayed, they all slumbered and slept. But at midnight there was a cry, "Behold! The bridegroom is coming! Come out to meet him!" Then all those virgins arose, and trimmed their lamps. The foolish said to the wise, "Give us some of your oil, for our lamps are going out." But the wise answered, saying, "What if there isn't enough for us and you? You go rather to those who sell, and buy for yourselves." While they went away to buy, the bride-groom came, and those who were ready went in with him to the wedding feast, and the door was shut. Afterward the other virgins also came, saying, "Lord, Lord, open to us." But he answered, "Most certainly I tell you, I don't know you." Watch therefore, for you don't know the day nor the hour in which the Son of Man is coming.[7]

Ashbery's playful expansion of this fable seems to take pity on the ostracized virgins—even coming to their defense in places—and imagines a kind of social architecture to the community of the household and its various servants. The piece is also in many ways a meditation on the nature of arrival, both in quotidian and spiritual terms. In our conversations about this manuscript, Ashbery's biographer, Karin Roffman, kindly pointed me toward Ashbery's early poem "A Sermon: Amos 8–11:14," which she discovered was written "the summer between his freshman and sophomore years" at Harvard on his family's farm in Sodus, NY.[8] This poem later appeared in *The Harvard Advocate*—his first poem published there—in April 1947.[9] "A Sermon: Amos 8–11:14" also mentions virgins and reflects on a passage of prophetic biblical verse. Roffman mentions this

---

7. Matt. 25:1–13, *World English Bible*.

8. Karin Roffman, *The Songs We Know Best: John Ashbery's Early Life*. Farrar, Straus and Giroux, 2017, 177.

9. Ibid.

poem in *The Songs We Know Best: John Ashbery's Early Life*, in connection with Ashbery's "religious period" at Harvard, quoting letters between Ashbery and his roommate, Bob Hunter:

> He vigorously defended his religious interests to his increasingly impatient friends. . . . Bob suspected that John's flirtation with religion was primarily a desire to resolve "the vast contradictions that existed within his soul." John argued that it was even more self-interested; at the very least, he said, it would "be a pity to be caught on the losing team on the Day of Atonement."[10]

J. S. Bach's 1731 cantata *Wachet auf, ruft uns die Stimme* (Sleepers Awake) is also based on the Matthew parable. Ashbery's sympathy for "sleepers" everywhere is well documented. A list poem titled "Sleepers Awake" appears in *Can You Hear, Bird* (1995): "I sleep when I cannot avoid it; my writing and sleeping are constantly improving."[11]

Additionally, Roffman observed that "ATTAINDER" and "Sacred and Profane Dances" bear narrative resemblance to another canonical surprise homecoming, the scenes in the *Odyssey* in which Odysseus returns to Ithaca and his former household, slaying Penelope's suitors—and Telemachus hangs the enslaved women who slept with them.[12]

ATTAINDER (85)

Ashbery typed the first two paragraphs of this poem on a single page, made corrections by hand, then retyped the page on a separate sheet, making further unmarked corrections and adding the third and fourth paragraphs, ending with "What is it about the bridegroom." He wrote the next passage, beginning "While

---

10. Ibid., 140–41.

11. John Ashbery, "Sleepers Awake," *Can You Hear, Bird*, in *John Ashbery: Collected Poems, 1991–2000*, ed. Mark Ford. Library of America, 2017, 484–85.

12. Karin Roffman, email to ES, May 4, 2020.

he was away, chaos under the guise of calm reigned in the house," on a separate page, which carries on to another. Since Ashbery seemed to be having some trouble with his typewriter here (the beginnings of some passages extend into the margin), I've made editorial choices for paragraph breaks throughout this section.

85: *"Maldoror considered these things, shifting his weight from haunch to haunch, then went over to the corner to question the view from his terrace."*

This is the first and only mention of Maldoror, the delightfully evil and nihilistic protagonist of one of Ashbery's favorite works of literature, *Les Chants de Maldoror* (1868–69), a novel in the form of a series of prose poetry cantos written by the Comte de Lautréamont (Isidore Lucien Ducasse). Ashbery first read *Les Chants de Maldoror* in the summer of 1950 in New York City.[13] In his review of a 1966 publication of Giorgio de Chirico's *Hebdomeros*, "The Decline of the Verbs," later reprinted as an introduction to the book, Ashbery compares *Les Chants de Maldoror* to de Chirico's novel: "Unlike the hero of Lautréamont's *Chants de Maldoror*, who is committed to evil, he [Hebdomeros] is uncommitted."[14] Ashbery then goes on to describe Lautréamont's novel as possessing "insane beauty," though ultimately lacking the "persuasion" of de Chirico's work.[15]

The shifts in narrator, point of view, and even sympathies that occur across and within these pieces also recall *Maldoror*'s roving narrative locus. Ashbery titled his 1992 collection of poems *Hotel Lautréamont*, in homage to the writer whose description of a sixteen-year-old boy has come to so succinctly capture the ethos of surrealism and assemblage: "He is fair ... as the chance meeting on a dissecting-table of a sewing-machine and an umbrella!"[16]

---

13. Karin Roffman, email to ES, Apr. 6, 2020.

14. John Ashbery, "Introduction, The Decline of the Verbs," *Hebdomeros*, Giorgio de Chirico. Exact Change, 1992, x.

15. Ibid., xi.

16. Comte de Lautréamont, *Maldoror*, in *Maldoror & the Complete Works of the Comte de Lautréamont*, trans. Alexis Lykiard. Exact Change, 2011, 193.

Sacred and Profane Dances (90)

This title was also used for a poem in *Your Name Here* (2000). *Danses sacrée et profane* (1904) is a work by Claude Debussy for harp and strings.

91: *"Why, though? Aren't they part of this whole household picture?"*

Ashbery retyped and subtly corrected the paragraph beginning with these sentences on the subsequent typescript page before continuing on.

Tempest (93)

94: *"whose volumes of Opie Read and F. Hopkinson Smith had remained untouched for almost a century,"*

Opie Read (1852–1939) was an American journalist and novelist; Francis Hopkinson Smith (1838–1915) was an American engineer, illustrator, and author. It is plausible that a stuffy American family of certain "conservative advanced taste," such as the fictional Wildwoods, would have these authors represented on their shelves.

APPENDIX D: 21 VARIATIONS

ON MY ROOM

Photocopies of this long poem were found in both of Ashbery's homes. In NYC, the poem was inside a folder with a note from Kermani: "JA poems 2003— NOT yet typed up / (these are ms copies) + 1 orig." Kermani penciled "[unfinished]," on the upper right-hand corner of the poem's first page. The one original typescript contained in the folder is a single quintet titled "Faded Ugliness," written in late 2003 or early 2004, that Ashbery indicated was not to be published. The Hudson photocopy, found in a folder marked "JA Xeroxes of poems," was among misfit photocopies from the early '90s-00s, including early photocopied drafts of his long poem "Heavenly Days."[1] It also contains typed and handwritten changes and corrections not present on the NYC photocopy.

Ashbery wrote "21 Variations on My Room" between August 21 and September 9, 2002. Incidentally, this was during his longest hiatus from writing *The Kane Richmond Project*, August 19 to November 9, 2002. According to his datebooks, this period was incredibly busy for Ashbery, including travel and readings for programs celebrating his seventy-fifth birthday "at the Pompidou Center in Paris (. . . organized by Olivier Brossard and Omar Berrada) and the Tate Modern in London" that fall, and even outpatient surgery during the summer.[2, 3] This poem, written just a few weeks before Ashbery and Kermani left for Paris, shares a source text with *The Kane Richmond Project*: *Tom Swift and His Rocket Ship* (1954), the third book in the serial Tom Swift novels for boys written by Victor

---

1. Published in John Ashbery, *Chinese Whispers*. Farrar, Straus and Giroux, 2002.

2. David Kermani, email to ES, Nov. 27, 2019.

3. Mark Ford and David Kermani, Chronology, in *John Ashbery: Collected Poems, 1991–2000*, ed. Mark Ford. Library of America, 2017, 783.

Appleton II, a collective name for the Stratemeyer Syndicate, which also published the Nancy Drew, Hardy Boys, and Bobbsey Twins serial novels.[4] In addition to *Tom Swift and His Rocket Ship*, Ashbery collaged material from two other Tom Swift/Hardy Boys novels into *The Kane Richmond Project* (see Appendix E). Because the two poems also share an Apollinaire epigraph and other language, "21 Variations on My Room" may have been conceived as part of the longer poem.

The number of lines in each stanza (with some exceptions) increase incrementally to more or less match the stanza's number. Only eighteen of the proposed "21 Variations" are completed.

In his long poem "And the Stars Were Shining," Ashbery writes: "Rummaging through some old poems / for ideas—surely I must have had some / once?"[5] Years after leaving "21 Variations on My Room" unfinished, Ashbery returned to it for inspiration, integrating many of its sections into "The Handshake, the Cough, the Kiss," published in his 2007 collection *A Worldly Country*. Though these two poems share much of their language, I have decided to include "21 Variations on My Room" in this collection. From a formal perspective, "21 Variations on My Room" creates a completely different reading experience from "The Handshake, the Cough, the Kiss," with its numbered sections and stanzaic constraints. The poem also sheds light on Ashbery's process of writing longer poems in his late career; the transition from the segmented form of "21 Variations . . ." to the seamlessness of "The Handshake . . ." is interesting to consider in terms of his compositional process and habit of self-recycling. Its connections to both this beloved long poem from *A Worldly Country* and *The Kane Richmond Project* mark it as an intriguing fulcrum in Ashbery's late writing.

99: [Epigraph] "Ma chambre a la forme d'une cage. —*Guillaume Apollinaire, 'Hôtel'*"

---

4. Victor Appleton II, *Tom Swift and His Rocket Ship*, ser. 3. Grosset & Dunlap, 1954.

5. John Ashbery, "And the Stars Were Shining," *And the Stars Were Shining*, in *John Ashbery: Collected Poems, 1991–2000*, 409.

"My room looks like a cage"[6]: This epigraph is not present on the photocopy of the poem found in NYC, but appears on the Hudson photocopy; Ashbery may have photocopied the original typescript to bring to NYC and later, in Hudson, typed the epigraph directly onto the photocopy. This epigraph also begins "A Long and Sleepy History," the seventeenth section of *The Kane Richmond Project*, which predates this poem. Additionally, Ashbery used this quote as an epigraph for the poem "Counterpane."[7]

100: **6.** If we follow the poem's formal logic, we might expect six lines here instead of five.

102: **12.** With thirteen lines instead of twelve, this stanza also breaks from the form of incrementally increasing lines per stanza.

102–3: **13.** This section is doubled, consisting of two thirteen-line stanzas.

104: **15.** *"One has to endure / certain systems, then profit by them later in the crust of events."*

The NYC photocopy of the poem has "evening" as the last word of this stanza. In the only original correction on the Hudson photocopy (other than the addition of the epigraph), Ashbery changed this word to "events."

105: **18.** *"I don't know—spring came and went so fast this year, / sex on the river— the chosen advice. And more."*

These lines appear, in slight variation, in the chapter "Sex on the River" in *The Kane Richmond Project*.

106: *"After that is the supervisors' area / and you could go home now, except they are expected here / and, wonderful to behold,"*

Save for the first few lines ("I don't know—spring came and went so fast this

---

6. Guillaume Apollinaire, "Hotel," *Zone: Selected Poems*, trans. Ron Padgett. New York Review Books, 2015, 131.

7. John Ashbery, *Where Shall I Wander*. Ecco/HarperCollins, 2005.

7

year ... and one observes it."), this is the only additional language supplied by Ashbery in this final stanza. The remaining material was collaged from pages 36–37 of *Tom Swift and His Rocket Ship*, a source Ashbery indicated with a typed note.[8]

106: "'*I hope we get the rest of the day off, genius boy,' Bud said shyly.*"
The final line substitutes "shyly" for the *Tom Swift and His Rocket Ship*'s "slyly."

---

8. See fig. 7.

APPENDIX E: THE KANE

RICHMOND PROJECT

On March 19, 2002, Ashbery printed a particularly handsome photograph of serial actor Kane Richmond he found on the internet. Two days later, he printed a filmography for Richmond, along with an article from *Images* journal, a "noncommercial Web site created for everyone who enjoys movies and popular culture."[1] The journal's fourth issue was dedicated to the subject of cliffhangers, and here Ashbery found an article by contributing editor Grant Tracey on *Spy Smasher*, a 1942 Republic Pictures Corporation serial directed by William Witney and starring Richmond as the cape-wearing, Nazi-busting superhero vigilante, whose true identity is Alan Armstrong, a war correspondent (Richmond also plays Spy Smasher's twin brother, Jack Armstrong). Tracey's enthusiasm for the serial is remarkable—every other sentence seems to end with an exclamation mark—and this three-page article, with its plot summaries of the various chapters, photographs, and analyses of the series' finer shots, became an important source for Ashbery, who even used the index of other articles from the issue (e.g., "Perils of Nyoka") as chapter titles. Also in Ashbery's possession was volume four of *Serial Pictorial*, a pulp fanzine from the late 1960s comprised of film stills and photographs from *Spy Smasher*.[2] On the front cover is Kane Richmond, half-smiling in his costume. These materials were found in Ashbery's study in NYC, in the desk drawer where he regularly kept files on ongoing projects and areas of curiosity.

Ashbery owned many film reference books, which he may have consulted in the writing of this poem. These included *Cliffhanger: A Pictorial History of the*

---

1. Grant Tracey, Elizabeth Abele, David Ng, and Craig Fischer, eds., *Images*, pub. Gary Johnson, www.imagesjournal.com/about.htm.

2. See figs. 13, 14, and 15.

Motion Picture Serial by Alan G. Barbour (1977), *A Pictorial History of the Silent Screen* by Daniel Blum (1953), *Harold Lloyd: The Man on the Clock* by Tom Dardis (1983), *Continued Next Week: A History of the Moving Picture Serial* by Kalton C. Lahue (1964), and *To Be Continued . . . : A Complete Guide to Motion Picture Serials* by Ken Weiss and Ed Goodgold (1972).[3]

Kane Richmond was a B-movie actor, best known for his appearance in serial films such as *The Shadow* and *Brick Bradford*. In this poem, Ashbery weaves together plotlines and characters from two of Richmond's other serials, *The Adventures of Rex and Rinty* (1935) and *Spy Smasher*, along with numerous allusions to other films from the 1920s, '30s, and '40s.

In two long poems from Ashbery's early career, he used text taken directly from books for adolescents. "Europe," the notoriously "inaccessible" 111-section poem published in *The Tennis Court Oath* (1962), contains long passages from *Beryl of the Biplane: Being the Romance of an Air-woman of To-day* (1917). Ashbery described the novel as a

> circa WWI book for young teenage girls . . . by William Le Queux, who was once a very successful English fiction writer. I found the book in a bookstall on the Seine and brought it home, planning to use it, but I didn't know how yet. It became an important element in my Europe "worldview," perhaps a further sign of orneriness on my part because it is mostly set in England, which is not really a part of Europe, as we know.[4]

---

3. For a complete listing of these film reference books, along with other books in Ashbery's library, see Rosangela Briscese and Micaela Morrissette's online bibliographic catalog of Ashbery's Hudson library. Rosangela Briscese and Micaela Morrissette, "Where Created Spaces Intersect: A Preliminary Inventory of John Ashbery's Personal Library," *A Dream of This Room: A Created Spaces Portfolio of Works on John Ashbery's Textual and Domestic Environments*, 2008, www.raintaxi.com/literary-features/john-ashbery-created -spaces/where-created-spaces-intersect/.

4. John Ashbery, transcript of handwritten annotations to *The Tennis Court Oath* (1962) for PEN America/First Editions, Second Thoughts, Mar.–Apr. 2014. Transcribed by ES.

Ashbery lifted long prose passages from *Beryl of the Biplane*, placing them, without context, among diffuse and abstract numbered sections. Of section 77, which reads in full, "'Perhaps you've heard of her. She's a great flying woman.' // 'Oh yes,' replied the stranger. 'I've seen things about / her in the papers. Does she fly much?'"[5] Ashbery recounted that these lines, quotes from the novel, are "fragments of conversation about the heroine from spies who are tracking her."[6]

Another poem that collages text from books written for children is "The Skaters," the long poem that ends the 1966 collection *Rivers and Mountains*, in which Ashbery included text from the 1911 hobby book, *Three Hundred Things a Bright Boy Can Do*, by "Many Hands." This user's guide for early twentieth-century boyhood features illustrated, highly detailed instructional chapters ranging from "Paperchasing, Football, Golf, and Boxing," to "Butterflies and Moths," and "Ventriloquism and Polyphony." David Shapiro, in a chapter dedicated entirely to the poem in *John Ashbery: An Introduction to the Poetry*, describes "The Skaters" as "a modulated collage on the ambiguous amusements of solitary mind."[7, 8]

In *The Kane Richmond Project*, Ashbery repeats this collage process, integrating language from three serialized novels for boys from the Tom Swift and Hardy Boys adventure series: *Tom Swift and His Rocket Ship* (1954) and *Tom Swift and His Repelatron Skyway* (1963), by Victor Appleton II; and *Danger on Vampire Trail*,

---

5. John Ashbery, "Europe," *The Tennis Court Oath*, in *John Ashbery: Collected Poems, 1956–1987*, ed. Mark Ford. Library of America, 2008, 106.

6. Ashbery, transcript of handwritten annotations to *The Tennis Court Oath* (1962).

7. I encourage readers interested in seeing the original typescript of "The Skaters," its first and second drafts, along with an impressive critical edition of the text (including "semantic annotations," "quantitative data analysis," and "searchable index") to seek out the incredible web-based "critical and genetic digital edition" of "The Skaters," created and conceived by Robin Seguy and Charles Bernstein for Text/*works*, a project supported by the University of Pennsylvania at www.text-works.org/Texts/Ashbery/JA-Sk_data/JA-Sk_EdN.html.

8. David Shapiro, *John Ashbery: An Introduction to the Poetry*. Columbia University Press, 1979, 93.

by Franklin W. Dixon (1971).[9, 10] A fourth book found with these texts, *Tom Swift and the Cosmic Astronauts* (1960), was not used. Dixon and Appleton are house pseudonyms for the Stratemeyer Syndicate, which also published the Nancy Drew and Bobbsey Twins serial novels, among others. Ashbery's use of these books marks a return to a previous source. In his critical study *On the Outside Looking Out: John Ashbery's Poetry*, John Shoptaw notes that after Ashbery wrote "Europe" in 1958, he used a Hardy Boys novel, *The Secret of the Old Mill*, to create a "puzzle-poem" with the same title on a seven-page grid of 36 squares.[11]

Ashbery's editions of these books once belonged to the personal libraries of Richard "Richie" E. Holland and Danny Klonsky. They were priced at $1 apiece; Ashbery may have bought them at Rodgers Book Barn in Hillsdale, NY, a famously treasure-packed used bookstore run by Maureen Rodgers that he loved and frequented. It is clear why Ashbery would have been attracted to these books: they are ripe for the collagist, with their imaginative inventions, over-the-top dialogue and character names, and humorous descriptions. In addition to being serialized novels, they also employ a cliffhanger structure between chapters, similar to the movie serials Ashbery references.

It bears mentioning that there are multiple moments of orientalism and racialized othering in *The Kane Richmond Project*. Because this associative poem evokes and collages the landscapes, plotlines, and characters of early Hollywood cinema and midcentury children's literature, it is difficult to say when this rhetoric is being directly deployed and when it is being parodied or otherwise repurposed. I personally feel that the reproduction of this language is unfortunate

---

9. See fig. 13.

10. Victor Appleton II, *Tom Swift and His Rocket Ship*, ser. 3. Grosset & Dunlap, 1954; Victor Appleton II, *Tom Swift and His Repelatron Skyway*, ser. 22. Grosset & Dunlap, 1963; Franklin W. Dixon, *The Hardy Boys: Danger on Vampire Trail*, ser. 50. Grosset & Dunlap, 1971.

11. John Shoptaw, *On the Outside Looking Out: John Ashbery's Poetry*. Harvard University Press, 1994, 359.

and—whatever Ashbery's intentions—participates in a colonialist, Eurocentric literary tradition of using the nonwhite figure as a nameless feature of the landscape or a placeholder for non sequitur, mystery, and indecipherability. To my knowledge, only a few scholars have taken up this aspect of Ashbery's writing: Stephen Ross discusses Ashbery's use of orientalism in the context of his fascination with "badness" in his book *Invisible Terrain: John Ashbery and the Aesthetics of Nature* (Oxford University Press, 2017). Kevin Killian wrote about racial stereotyping in Ashbery's plays.[12] I believe this facet of Ashbery's writing deserves further attention.

Readers may notice some reappearance of phrases throughout the poem, instances of which I have made an attempt to note. Additionally, there are recurrences of language between this poem and "21 Variations on My Room." These repetitions are not unusual for Ashbery, who was known in his drafts and published work to reuse lines (and even titles) across several poems, since he often worked from fragments written on scraps of paper. Sometimes, he would forget already having used a fragment in another poem, or would want to try it somewhere else in a different context.[13] On a larger scale, three poems from Ashbery's collection *And the Stars Were Shining* (1994) appeared, sometimes in slight variation or with differing titles, in *Can You Hear, Bird* (1995). This repetition of material was a conscious element of his collage work—as the same image could induce drastically different effects in different contexts, such as Pieter Bruegel the Elder's *Tower*[s] *of Babel*, the pastel macaron cookie cutouts sprinkled throughout Ashbery's later collages, or the reappearance of Parmigianino's *Self-*

---

12. Kevin Killian, "Ashbery's Theater: 'Three Plays' (1978)," *Conjunctions*, John Ashbery Tribute, eds. Peter Gizzi and Bradford Morrow, 49 (2007): 334–40.

13. Around the late 1990s or early 2000s, Ashbery and Kermani became frustrated by how long it was taking to find unwanted repetitions in the poem drafts, and decided that Kermani should place a checkmark next to fragments that had been used in a draft, and, on the verso of the fragment, note the date on which the corresponding poem was written; the intent was not to stop the repetitions, but merely to make it easier to locate them so Ashbery could decide which to retain and which to change.

portrait in a Convex Mirror in varying sizes across many years of collage-making. In his visual art, these recurrences were a way of uniting a group of collages, creating visual and referential conversations within a body of work. But as a poet, Ashbery would sometimes seek out and remove these repeated moments from a manuscript. In *The Kane Richmond Project*, among other noticeable patterns of repetition, quotes from the body of the poem often reappear later as chapter titles, producing an interesting, regenerative effect.

As for the physical manuscript itself, the original typescripts and corresponding photocopies were found in a manila folder in the same file drawer in the NYC apartment as *The Art of Finger Dexterity*. A note by Kermani placed at the beginning of the folder of manuscript material explains that some pages were, at some point, separated and lost (and later recovered), which might illuminate some of the erratic ordering and discrepancies with regard to section breaks. There are multiple copies: original typescripts, photocopies with handwritten changes by Ashbery, and a final copy assembled on May 21, 2003, by Kermani, in which, according to a note on the separate folder in which this copy of the manuscript was stored, "only [the] most recent revised pages" are present.

This manuscript presented many editorial challenges. Because Ashbery wrote from both Hudson and NYC and wanted photocopies in both locations (and sometimes made additional photocopies when he traveled elsewhere), multiple drafts with different variants exist. There are misordered pages, several undated entries, and handwritten pages, and a pattern emerged wherein Ashbery began new passages out of sequence underneath previous entries or on their own pages, with no indication of whether or not he wanted a section break. Luckily, Kermani's meticulously annotated and assembled final copy, along with Ashbery's practice of dating his entries, made it possible to reconstruct a version of *The Kane Richmond Project* that might resemble Ashbery's vision. What emerges is a collaged, hybrid, and exciting homage to the serial form.

Toward the end of the typescript, Ashbery stopped indicating breaks in the text at the top of the page. In some places, even when indicated, it is unclear whether Ashbery intended a break at the top or bottom of the page, or whether "break" means stanza/paragraph break or section break. At these cruxes, I considered the overall function of the "break" in this poem, with its many titled chapters, and how a break, for the poet, can act as its own cliffhanger or rupture in narrative or image. In these formal considerations and decisions, I have tried, instead of "tidying up," to make choices that leave the text as open as possible to the many possibilities in formatting and form. Here, untitled sections, indicated in the text by three asterisks (* * *), signify page breaks in the typescript, which because of long periods of time elapsed between entries or space left at the bottom of the previous page, I could not determine to be either section breaks or stanza/paragraph breaks.

According to a note by Kermani on a photocopy of the first page of the original typescript, Ashbery made many of the handwritten changes in April 2003, four months after he completed his last entry. Though a note by Kermani tucked into one of the Tom Swift books in order to link it with this poem refers to *The Kane Richmond Project* as "unfinished," it reads as though it has a beginning, middle, and end. The only steps that remained were integrating Ashbery's changes and making some decisions regarding formatting and structure. I felt honored to facilitate this part of the process.

A note on the title: In a document labeled "(DRAFT) Alphabetical List of JA Poems: Late 2001–2002 (as of 5/15/03)," this project is referred to as *Spy Smasher; The Kane Richmond Project*. Ashbery indicated that he was considering *Spy Smasher* as a title for the full manuscript on a photocopy of the first page, circling "Spy Smasher," the first chapter title underneath the title *The Kane Richmond Project*, and writing "Change title?"[14] next to it. On the first page of the original typescript, Ashbery even circled "Spy Smasher" and drew an arrow above *The Kane Richmond Project*. Ashbery also considered *The Kane Richmond Story*, writing "Story?" above "Project" on the photocopy of the first page.[15] Since I could find no definitive preference, I kept to Ashbery's original title.

---

14. See fig. 8.
15. Ibid.

Spy Smasher (117)

Ashbery proposed this as an alternate title for the manuscript.

Perils of Nyoka (119)

Ashbery titled this chapter "Perils of Inoka." However, *Perils of Nyoka* is the 1942 serial, also directed by William Witney, listed on Ashbery's source material (with the correct spelling), directly underneath *Spy Smasher*. Since Ashbery may have unintentionally transposed the consonant and vowel sounds of "ny" and "in," I corrected the chapter title to reflect his source.

The Devil Diamond (119)

This title, along with *The Lost City*, *Racing Blood*, *Spy Smasher*, and *The Adventures of Rex and Rinty* (not used as a chapter title but referenced throughout the poem), appears on the printout of Kane Richmond's filmography found in Ashbery's study. Ashbery indicated that he was thinking about beginning the poem with this section, writing "begin here?" in the left margin and drawing a line toward this chapter title.

The Devil Diamond (1937) is a film directed by Leslie Goodwins and starring Kane Richmond as Jerry Carter, an undercover detective who is hired to keep tabs on a large diamond that is coveted by thieves and rumored to be cursed.

119: *"and huge morsel of bone for Bonzo"*
Bonzo the Dog is a 1920s cartoon character illustrated by George Studdy, a British comic artist.

The Lost City (121)

The Lost City (1935) is an unwatchable sci-fi serial starring Richmond as engineer Bruce Gordon.

Racing Blood (122)

Richmond plays a handsome stable owner in *Racing Blood* (1936), a film directed by Victor Halperin about a "crippled colt" that grows up to be a racing champion at the center of a web of racetrack-related crime and deception.

124: *"'Dear' had life tinged on it? Not on my watch, / they don't. It was so casual of you, too."*

These lines begin the top of the fifth typescript page, labeled "KRP 5 stanza break," indicating Ashbery wanted a stanza break between this and what came before on the previous page. The word "dear" is lowercase, and Ashbery wrote "missing page?" in pen above the text, likely because the first word isn't capitalized. The last line of the previous page, "That's what it's coming to, to true blue," ends in a period. It makes sense that "'dear' had life" is here because of the appearance of the phrase in the first stanza of "Racing Blood": "started bailing for dear life. 'Dear' life?"[16] but since this lack of capitalization confused even Ashbery, I've capitalized the first word of this stanza.

125: *"Rudy is shanghaied aboard the Lady Letty / and falls for Moran, the captain's daughter. / Soon the kindly captain dies. Rudy's rich friends / have forgotten him, though he dreams of them. / Here, do it like this. / No, like this."*

Here, Ashbery is referring to *Moran of the Lady Letty* (1922), an American silent film starring Dorothy Dalton as Moran, the resourceful daughter of a Norwegian sea captain, and silent-era heartthrob Rudolph Valentino as Ramon

---

16. *Parallel Movement of the Hands*, 122.

Laredo, a member of San Francisco's upper class. The film also includes a performance by Japanese actor George Kuwa. As with Ashbery's use of "Kane," the character carries the actor's name, "Rudy." An expository intertitle reads, "the rich man's son—Ramon Laredo—spends the dash and fire inherited from his Spanish ancestors in leading cotillions. . . . Cradled in luxury this man-child came to earth, heir to the aimless life of a rich man's son." On his way to a day of yachting hosted by his Nob Hill debutante love interest, Ramon is shanghaied by crew members of the *Heart of China*, a pirate ship passing through San Francisco Bay. A coal fire erupts on Moran's father's nearby ship, the *Lady Letty*, and all of the crew members (including its captain) expire in the noxious fumes. When sailors from the *Heart of China* arrive to pillage the ship, they find Moran alive, but think her to be a boy. When it is discovered that Moran is a woman, Ramon Laredo saves her from the advances of the captain. The two eventually fall in love, and Laredo gives up his swanky lifestyle, pledging his life to Moran and the open sea.

The film is particularly striking from a gender perspective. Moran is described as having been "reared as a hardy seaman. . . . Born on the deep and rocked to sleep by storms, this girl-child came of a long line of sea-faring men." When Laredo declares his love, Moran sighs, "I ought to have been born a boy." Laredo, on the other hand, is cruelly mocked by the captain in front of the crew for his softness and femininity, and is given the nickname "Lillee of the Vallee" on deck, a detail I can see Ashbery enjoying.

125: *"Rex and Rinty are a part / of the equation."*

This is the first mention of Rex and Rinty, the scrappy animal pals and co-conspiratorial duo of the twelve-part serial *The Adventures of Rex and Rinty* (1935). Rex, a black Arabian stallion played by equine actor Rex, King of the Wild Horses, lives on the island of Sujan, where the inhabitants worship him like a god, "cherishing him as sincerely as did the Assyrians the Bull; the Egyptians the Cat; or the Mayans the Feathered Serpent." Rex is stolen from the island by a gang of Americans and shipped to California, fated to become a polo horse. Rinty, played by canine actor Rin Tin Tin Jr., is a "homeless" Californian dog with "human intelligence." The two join forces to get Rex back home, helping to free each other from many perils in the process. This serial's human cast includes Kane Richmond as Frank Bradley, a "famed polo player," who helps Rex return to Sujan after he is held captive by villain Crawford and his accomplices. Rex and Rinty become repeated characters in Ashbery's poem, and their story lines often commingle with those of *Spy Smasher*.

This isn't the first time Ashbery drew inspiration from a film starring Rin Tin Tin. In her biography of Ashbery's early life, *The Songs We Know Best* (2017), Karin Roffman recounts his involvement in the Theodore Huff Memorial Film Society in the mid-1950s, and how his attendance inspired his play *The Compromise*:

> At the very first event, he found inspiration for a new play. After watching a two-minute hand-colored film from 1900 called *The Flower Fairy*, he also saw, for the first time, the classic, full-length Rin Tin Tin feature *Where the North Begins* (1923). Afterward, he rapturously described it to Kenneth [Koch] as "the greatest film ever—Rinty is a superb actor." The story is set on a remote mountain, where deep snow has left a small group in almost total isolation from the rest of society for much of the year. Rin Tin Tin, raised by wolves but with the old soul of a dog, provides a lonely young family with companionship, loyalty, and wisdom. Moved by the film, Ashbery went to work that night as soon as he arrived home.
>
> Less than three weeks later, he had a complete draft of his first three-act play.[17]

Ashbery also provided an account of seeing this film in an interview with Mark Ford:

> *The Compromise* was inspired by going to a film society that Edward Gorey belonged to, which was sort of semi-clandestine, as if they didn't really want

---

17. Karin Roffman, *The Songs We Know Best: John Ashbery's Early Life*. Farrar, Straus and Giroux, 2017, 234.

people to come, and it moved around from one space to another. They showed very strange unknown films—it was run by William K. Everson, an English film scholar who lived in New York. *The Compromise* was inspired by a 1923 Rin Tin Tin movie I saw there, *Where the North Begins*. I took the plot of this movie, though I omitted the dog at the centre of it. This dog had been left to guard a baby in a trappers' cabin while the parents are out; they come back and find the baby missing and the whole place torn apart—in fact by the furious fight the dog had with the baby's kidnappers, but the parents wrongly conclude that the dog has eaten the baby, and cast the poor mutt out into the snow! There was something about this film which intrigued me—maybe because it was made just before I was born, around the time my parents got married, and I saw something of my parents in both of the leading actors, though I've no idea now who they were.[18]

126: *"Goran stabs the horse fatally, and police in riot gear / converge on the scene."*
It is unclear here whether Ashbery meant to write "Moran," the female lead in *Moran of the Lady Letty*.

126: *"That's the president's dream"*
Ashbery titled a later chapter "The President's Dream."

127: *"'Society figure' (that would be Rudy) 'missing: foul play feared.' / What about our crimes and delusions? Haven't we walked the plank far enough?"*
This refers to a scene in *Moran of the Lady Letty* in which Laredo's socialite girlfriend is reading headlines about his disappearance in the newspaper.

128: *"I have researched my position paper / to the fullest, and am ready to pronounce: / Big music in mid-disaster."*
Ashbery titled a poem "Position Paper" in his collection *Breezeway* (2015).

128: *"Rex and Rinty were never the same / after the burning stable incident, but did either of them let out a growl / or as much as a whimper?"*

---

18. John Ashbery and Mark Ford, *John Ashbery in Conversation with Mark Ford*. Between the Lines, 2003, 36–37.

A direct reference to a cliffhanger in the third chapter of *The Adventures of Rex and Rinty*, "Fangs of Flame," in which the barn where Crawford's men are holding Rex catches fire after one of them drops a cigarette on a bale of hay. Richmond's character, Frank Bradley, rushes in to save Rinty and the stolen horse from the fire and (in the next chapter) frees Rex from the horse thieves.

130–31: *"The real test came though when Rinty found Kane all tied up like that. / In a flash he knew what to do—chew through the cords so Kane could reach his holster, / and nary a moment too soon—the Gestapo guy returned / to the cell. 'Vell, haf you considered the terms of my—' / Whop! in a moment Rinty was all over him, Kane kicked over the bales / of straw and ignited them and escaped through the door with Rinty / to the tunnel the Gestapo guy had left open, slamming the door behind them. / Now he was free to rejoin his twin brother, / he of the gorgeous tweeds, in the sky, in an airship floating over Paris."*

This is a conflation of scenes from *Spy Smasher* (part of which is set in Nazi-occupied Paris) and *The Adventures of Rex and Rinty*.

The President's Dream (132)

A short, undated chapter, written sometime between April 13 and 20, 2002. It begins on the bottom of the eighth typescript page, and continues onto the top of the ninth, after which there is much blank space.

[untitled] "Kane was a righteous dude, heat-packing." (133)

This passage begins on a page that Ashbery originally labeled "KRP 8 - break." The "8" is crossed out and replaced by a "9" on the original typescript, which is then replaced by a "10" in the final copy. This is the first in a series of mislabeled pages throughout the typescripts, perhaps due to Ashbery forgetting to number his pages, or because of pages getting misordered or temporarily misplaced during relocations between Hudson and NYC. Up until this point, chapters have been separated by titles, much like the chapters in the serial films to which Ashbery refers. In this case, since the passage on the previous page was undated and much space remained at the bottom of the page, I've treated this passage as its own, untitled chapter and maintained Ashbery's section break (not his page break), as I do several times throughout the poem.

133: *"He preferred the poetry of Charlotte Mew to that of Nathalia Crane,"*

Charlotte Mew (1869–1928) was an English poet, known for her poem "The Farmer's Bride." Nathalia Crane (1913–1998) was an American novelist and poet who published *The Janitor's Boy*, her first poetry collection, when she was just eleven.

134: *"The sky was dark as coagulated blood. / 'Halleluljah! They must think I'm daft / not to notice what's going on behind. / Here, I think I'll fake a snooze, and then …'"*

I initially corrected this strange spelling of "Hallelujah," but then reverted it to Ashbery's original spelling, thinking it could perhaps be intentional, indicating a regional accent. Rosanne Wasserman pointed me to a 1928 recording by Harry McClintock of the popular folk song "Hallelujah! I'm a Bum," in which the word is indeed pronounced this way, with an additional "ul" lilting in the middle of the word.[19]

135: *"In a cellar somewhere in Paris the scratchy sounds / of the TSF had made their point, though."*

TSF is an acronym for *Télécoms Sans Frontières*, a French nongovernmental organization providing emergency communications during times of crisis.

135: *"Kane was lost in the Métro, / somewhere between Plaisance and Pernety."*

This phrase begins a page that Ashbery originally labeled "KRP 9 no break." In subsequent drafts, the "9" is crossed out and replaced with a "10," and the "10" is crossed out and replaced with an "11."[20] Although Ashbery wrote "no

---

19. Rosanne Wasserman, conversation with ES, Dec. 19, 2019.

20. See fig. 9.

break," it seems that a natural break occurs between the last line of the previous page ("Soon it would be time to break out the champagne again.") and the line that begins page 11 ("Kane was lost in the Métro"). Because the pagination is confused, I have inserted a stanza break here.

Ashbery cut a version of these lines a few pages earlier, from the end of "The President's Dream." After "Can we take their irrelevance seriously?"[21] Ashbery initially wrote "Gaps in the Metro—Plaisance and Pernety. Women who smoke / and haunt the *fortifs*."

135: *"They puzzled over a chart / thought to be of importance."*

The last line of this section ("And then said nothing more.") originally followed this line, but Ashbery moved it to the end of the section in a subsequent draft.[22]

136: *"'The moon doth shine as bright as day,'"*

This is a line from the eighteenth-century nursery rhyme "Girls and Boys Come Out to Play":

> Girls and boys, come out to play,
> The moon doth shine as bright as day;
> Leave your supper, and leave your sleep,
> And come with your playfellows into the street.
> Come with a whoop, come with a call,
> Come with a good will or not at all.
> Up the ladder and down the wall,
> A halfpenny roll will serve us all.
> You find milk, and I'll find flour,
> And we'll have a pudding in half an hour.[23]

---

21. *Parallel Movement of the Hands*, 133.

22. See fig. 9.

23. J. O. Halliwell-Phillipps, *The Nursery Rhymes of England: Collected Chiefly from Oral Tradition*. J. R. Smith, 1846, 203.

Chapter Seven (136)

This is actually the eighth chapter title in the poem, not the seventh.

136: *"Mme. Delaunay brought out the redingote she'd knitted before the war and placed it sideways on a chair, it caught the sun's declining rays."*

Here Ashbery is referring to the Russian-born Parisian painter Sonia Delaunay, a figure associated with the Orphism movement. Delaunay was also a textile and costume designer, which explains the description of a gorgeous and impossible garment that follows.

The Mist Rolls in from the Sea (137)

137–38: *"Tin lizzies were slamming around the neat suburban streets in the Harold Lloyd movie, past lawns and houses that looked newer than 1923."*

Harold Lloyd was an American silent-film-era comedic actor and stuntman. The film referred to here is likely the comedic romance *Safety Last* (1923), with its iconic "human fly" scene of Lloyd hanging from the hands of a skyscraper's large exterior clock.

Dog and Pony Show (139)

Ashbery wrote "begin here?" in the margin next to the title of this short, undated chapter.

A Lost Dog (140)

In the original typescript and subsequent photocopies, this section, written June 1–2, 2002, appears on its own page after a page containing three sections: "The Mist Rolls in from the Sea" (May 29, 2002), "Dog Overboard!" (June 3, 2002), and the three-sentence "Dog and Pony Show" (undated). Ashbery's dates indicate that he wrote "A Lost Dog" between "The Mist Rolls in from the Sea" and "Dog Overboard!" and that he returned to the previous page the following day to fill in the space he'd left blank underneath the earlier passage.

The text of the epigraph, from French Calvinist poet and historical writer Théodore-Agrippa d'Aubigné's autobiography, *His Life, to His Children*, has been corrected to match the original passage. Ashbery indicated his edition of the book and the page number with a note in the margin, "(Pléiade 406)."[24] In his 1989 translation of Aubigné's text, John Nothnagle renders this passage as

> Dominge, having fulfilled his vow, went to Agen, where he found his master playing handball with Laverdin. They stopped their game to question him. He spoke of the action [at Castel-Jaloux] with praise for his captain, not as extravagant as that of Bacoue, but more judicious, and thereby completely lost the friendship of his master as well as compensation for thirty-eight harquebus wounds that he had suffered. Note what the great men of this world turn their backs to, even the best of them.[25]

140: "'*He hides his face to become an evil spirit,*' *she explained. '*The medicine gourd is my sister Betty's, and the axe is the sign of Skip, the thunder god.*' // As the witch doctor danced, he began to chant and wail. His voice rose to a hideous shriek as he hopped about. '*That caterwaulin' alone could scare the wits out o' any critter,*' *Rinty reflected.*"

These quotes come from a passage in *Tom Swift and His Repelatron Skyway*. Ashbery indicated this source with the novel's title and the page number "(73)"

---

24. Théodore-Agrippa d'Aubigné, *Oeuvres*, ed. Henry Weber. Bibliothèque de la Pléiade. Paris, 1969.

25. Théodore-Agrippa d'Aubigné, *His Life, to His Children = Sa vie à ses enfants*, trans. John Nothnagle. University of Nebraska Press, 1989, 38–39.

alongside the date of the entry. Here, Ashbery has substituted "My sister Betty's" and "Skip" for the original text's "Uoshu's" and "Sho-sho-go," respectively.

141: *"They walked rapidly behind the hound, who kept his nose to the ground, with ears flapping. He stopped beside the steps of a small trailer. It was weirdly painted in psychedelic colors."*

Ashbery notes that this passage is taken from page 107 of the Hardy Boys novel, *Danger on Vampire Trail*.

My Own Best Customer (141)

The page on which this passage begins is one of the most mysterious in the typescripts. The original typescript page has a few handwritten changes, and subsequent photocopies of this page (of which there are three in the original manuscript folder) accumulated more changes and corrections, not all of which were carried over from draft to draft. The page was photocopied at least once *before* it was finished, leaving a half-completed copy under which Ashbery, five months later, began the entry starting "Are you trying to stop us?"[26] The timing of this sequencing error corresponds with Ashbery's return from a long trip to France and the UK for the celebration of his seventy-fifth birthday, during which time he did not work on *The Kane Richmond Project*. This passage was photocopied and relocated to its proper place in the typescripts by Kermani when he compiled the final copy.

On what appears to be the first photocopy of this passage (made from the completed original typescript page), Ashbery wrote and circled the chapter title "My own best customer" at the top. In subsequent drafts, on which additional handwritten changes were made, this insertion was not carried over. My first impulse was to not include this title, which does not appear on the final copy,

---

26. *Parallel Movement of the Hands*, 164.

but after researching the source of the phrase as it relates to Ashbery's life, I have decided to reinsert it.

In her article "This Comic Version of Myself," Karin Roffman mentions this phrase in relation to some of the humorous language in *A Nest of Ninnies* (1969):

> For Ashbery, it was his mother and her female friends who provided the material for some of the funniest lines in the novel.... Underlying these comments was a vision of the world that was tragic but accepting, but Ashbery learned to put his own ironic, witty spin on the kinds of things his mother and her friends said. For example, a Sodus friend, who owned an antique store, said one day to Ashbery: "I am my own best customer." The phrase was said straightforwardly, but Ashbery loved how it pithily explained her lack of business success, for her store was failing.[27]

The phrase "my own best customer" ends the first stanza of "Blueprints and Others," from Ashbery's collection *Breezeway* (2015): "The man across the street seems happy, / or pleased. Sometimes a porter evades the grounds. / After you play a lot with the military / you are my own best customer."[28]

144: "The Big Clock, The Big Knife, *and* The Big Sleep *were all playing, next to* The Big House. *Still, if you'd rather I'd ...*"

All initial letters in these four film titles are capitalized here, which was not consistent in the typescripts, and in italics, since Ashbery italicized film titles in later sections (e.g., *Think Fast, Mr. Moto*).

Ashbery owned a number of film guides and reference books on film. In a 2016 interview with scholar David Spittle about the influence of film and surrealism on his poetry, Ashbery responded, "I can't think of other books on film that have been important, except for the Hallowell guides and Leonard Maltin's

---

27. Karin Roffman, "This Comic Version of Myself: Humor and Autobiography in John Ashbery's Poetry and Prose," *Humor in Modern American Poetry*, ed. Rachel Trousdale. Bloomsbury Academic, 2018, 204.

28. John Ashbery, *Breezeway*. Ecco/HarperCollins, 2015, 64.

guides for catching films on TV. That book was useful when I wrote a poem, 'They Knew What They Wanted,' where every line was a movie title that began with 'they.'"[29] Ashbery may have gleaned this list of films from a similar guide.

145: "All right, John. John are you home? *I am a pack rat.*"
The phrase "I am a pack rat" also occurs in "A Long and Sleepy History."[30]

145: "*Both had a long and sleepy history. One came from where it had been aroused.*"
Ashbery titled a later chapter "A Long and Sleepy History."

Dog of the Limberlost (147)

A Girl of the Limberlost is a 1909 novel by American naturalist and author Gene Stratton-Porter, with several film adaptations.

148: "*Cheese—at the moment? Nutcases. / The night when you saw Screwy Squirrel / When I went over to him I said I'm sorry. / We respect these. // William Biggs died some years ago.*"
Ashbery originally ended this section with the line above these, "Nothing much comes to cheat us / of this vapor." Three days later, he fed a photocopy of the original typescript page through his typewriter, adding this last passage, which does not appear on subsequent drafts with Ashbery's corrections and changes. Thinking this omission was perhaps an error, and since the passage was not crossed out, I've included it.

---

29. John Ashbery and David Spittle, "An Interview with John Ashbery," *The Midnight Mollusc* (blog), Sep. 15, 2016, themidnightmollusc.blogspot.com/2016/09/an-interview-with-john-ashbery.html.

30. *Parallel Movement of the Hands*, 150.

Ashbery heavily edited this poem, cutting and rearranging stanzas, and combining, inverting, and excising lines on the undated typescript page. Many of the original lines were taken from *Danger on Vampire Trail*, though none survived in the revision. He indicates this with a note, "VT 1, 2," in the right margin.[31] Ashbery's copy of the novel originally belonged to a boy named Richie Holland, who wrote his name (in very nice cursive) in red ink on the title page. One could see why Ashbery would have been attracted to this book from the campy synopsis in its front matter:

> An assignment from their famous detective father to track down a ring of credit-card counterfeiters takes Frank and Joe Hardy on an exciting camping trip to the Rocky Mountains.
>
> The cross-country trek with their pals Chet Morton and Biff Hooper is jinxed from the very first day. Trouble with their tent trailer is compounded by vicious harassments all the way to Colorado. Here their enemies strike at Biff's loveable bloodhound in another attempt to scare the teen-age detectives off the case. In Denver a skein of clues confuses the Hardys. How many gangs are out to get them—one, two, or three?
>
> Strange happenings on a nearly impassable mountain lure Frank, Joe, Chet, and Biff to almost certain death before they discover the sinister reason for the danger on Vampire Trail.

Ashbery repeated some of the language in "Sex on the River" in section 18 of "21 Variations on My Room" (see Appendix D, entry for p. 105, *"I don't know— spring came and went so fast this year . . ."*).

I have added the attribution of the epigraph, James Tate's "The Wheelchair Butterfly," from his 1970 collection *The Oblivion Ha-Ha*. For the entire time I worked for him, Ashbery had a stack of Tate's books on the antique daybed in

---

31. See fig. 10.

the office in NYC where he wrote. He also kept a grouping of Tate's books near his workspace in his Hudson study.[32]

A Long and Sleepy History (150)

After this section, Ashbery, for the most part, stopped indicating at the top of pages whether there is a section, paragraph, or stanza break, so in many cases from this place forward, I've had to use contextual information to make an educated guess.

I have added information such as Stein's and Apollinaire's first names and the title of Apollinaire's poem, to the two epigraphs; the Apollinaire epigraph also begins "21 Variations on My Room."

150: "*Stepping into the little skiff one is quickly carried away to a land of impatient dreams.*"

Ashbery spelled the penultimate word in this sentence "ompaitnet," later indicating with a handwritten note that even he was unclear as to whether he meant to write "impatient" or "omnipotent." Both have their charms. At first, I leaned toward the latter, which is easier to misspell and carries the first letter of the original word. But "impatient" is in fact closer to the misspelled word and contains the same number of letters. In a preceding sentence, the river that will presumably carry one to this land of dreams is "impertinent," which, being a near homophone, would nicely foreshadow "impatient." The following sentence, "No, it's this way we wanted to come," struck me as particularly impatient, too.

150: "'*I* am *a pack rat,*' *one said, as though to reassure himself.*"

The phrase "I am a pack rat" occurs first in "My Own Best Customer."[33]

155: "*Meanwhile, the attention of the Americans was caught by a herd of lyre-horned Ankole cattle grazing on the grassy slopes. // 'Right smart-lookin' beeves,' Chow commented.*"

---

32. David Kermani, email to ES, Apr. 29, 2020.

33. *Parallel Movement of the Hands,* 145.

Ashbery indicated in a typed parenthetical, "(repelatron 58)," that this quotation is sourced from *Tom Swift and His Repelatron Skyway*.

The Quitter (156)

156: *"What amazes me is the lack / of a clue or anything resembling one, or / even an inkling such things can exist."*

This phrase recalls a line in the first stanza of Ashbery's poem "Breezeway," from his eponymous 2015 collection: "Alas it wasn't my call. / I didn't have a call or anything resembling one."[34]

Modern Sketch (158)

158: *"Sleep a weak hour"*

In the original typescript pages, passages of poetry are often indented further than prose sections. There is a typed "Slee" in the left margin (crossed out with a typewritten "XXXX"), suggesting Ashbery may have originally intended to begin this passage as prose.

158: *"air of Reynaldo Hahn: / 'C-est l'heure ... l'heure exquise'—sho'!"*

Reynaldo Hahn (1874–1947), born in Venezuela, was a French composer and singer beloved by many writers, including Mallarmé and Proust. "L'Heure exquise" ("The Exquisite Hour") is one of his most famous songs, its lyrics a poem by Paul Verlaine. Ashbery's collage *L'Heure Exquise* (1977) depicts a woman with a parrot perched on her knee. In the background are silhouettes of giant saguaro cacti in a lightning storm.

159: *"It is exactly where you left it. / I want out."*

There is no indication as to whether there should be a stanza break between

---

34. Ashbery, *Breezeway*, 14.

these two lines, which span a page break in the typescript. I chose not to insert a stanza break, as it seemed more in keeping with the patterning of lines per stanza (the following stanza is also seven lines, and there are no other three-line stanzas in this chapter).

159–60: *"If so, why bother / sober ascending / Apple Annie"*

Apple Annie is a character played by actress May Robson in the film comedy *Lady for a Day* (1933). Annie, a loud-mouthed, drunken apple seller on the streets of New York City, must disguise herself as a lady of society in order to fool her own daughter, who has been residing in a Spanish convent since Annie gave her up at birth and is coming to visit Annie on the occasion of her recent engagement. Annie has been corresponding with her daughter across the ocean under the false name Mrs. E. Worthington Manville, and maintains appearances for the reunion with help from her disreputable acquaintances.

To Meet with My Father (161)

This short chapter, written on July 20 and 21, 2002, occurs at the top of its own, unnumbered page. Since Ashbery wrote it only several days after the chapter ending on the previous page, I have inserted a chapter break, but not a page break, between this and the previous section. Given that there is extra space at the bottom of the page, I have also inserted a chapter break between "To Meet with My Father" and the entry that begins on the next typescript page.

161: *"Bud looked up in amazement."*

Ashbery indicated with a parenthetical, "(Swift Rocket, 149)," inserted in the middle of the paragraph, that this sentence is taken from *Tom Swift and His Rocket Ship*.

[untitled] *"I liked the fourth declension—all those 'u's."* (162)

I have placed a section break between this untitled passage and the previous chapter, "To Meet with My Father," because twenty-two days elapsed between the writing of these sections, and Ashbery did not indicate whether this new passage is part of the previous section or the beginning of its own. It was my hope that this choice might leave both possibilities open to the reader.

Miss Otis Regrets Land's End (163)

The title references a song for which Ashbery had a particular fondness. "Miss Otis Regrets" (1934) by Cole Porter was performed and revived by many singers. The song, a parody of the vigilante murder ballad, describes an upper-class woman who shoots a lover who has done her wrong. She is eventually caught, and, as she awaits her hanging, is forced to politely decline her lunch plans via a butler or doorman, who reports: "Miss Otis regrets she's unable to lunch today."

In an email to Mark Ford, dated January 23, 2012, Ashbery wrote:

> I'll also play you selections from my new CD of thirties British camp icon Douglas Byng, such as Songs of the Shires ("Nana of the Manor" is my favorite), and "Boadicea": "I'm just a keen old British queen who rules the countryside, / I never disregard me 'igh vocation!" It includes his rendition of Cole Porter's tragicomic "Miss Otis Regrets." I had 78 rpm's of them when I was at Harvard. Oh well, here's an unrequested snatch from the former, sung as if by "Old Nana, the keeper of the manor, In and out the lodge all day": "Now they say the manor's haunted, full of ghosts with eyes that shine. Well, I slept up there one Christmas—lots of guests, and lots of wine (giggle). But all I heard was gentle taps, on every door but mine! In and out the lodge all day!" Surely there must be an influence on "Are You Being Served?" of which we

just watched a prime example wherein Mrs. Slocombe takes to the bottle (an atomizer full of gin, for one) and imagines herself madly in love with Mr. Humphries.[35]

Ford and Ashbery continued a New York School epistolary tradition by signing and addressing their letters to each other with humorous names, and "Miss Otis" may well have been one of them. The exchange from which the above was taken produced the *noms de plume* "Peggy Popular," "Nana of the Manor," and "Boadicea," to name just a few.[36]

Sometimes, when Ashbery mentioned a song in an email he was dictating that was unfamiliar to me, he would invite me to play it on the stereo or pull it up on the laptop. On special occasions, he would sing along gloriously.

164: *"What the, she's happy. And so arse we—just don't know it yet."*

The typescript originally reads "And so are we," but Ashbery (thankfully) changed "are" to "arse."

[untitled] *"Are you trying to stop us?"* (164)

I have treated this passage as its own chapter so as not to make assumptions regarding Ashbery's structural wishes. On November 9, Ashbery began this passage underneath an old, partial photocopy of what became "My Own Best Customer" (see entry for p. 141, "My Own Best Customer"). Only entries from June 4–5, 2002, were present when this photocopy was made, before the June 10 entry was added. When Kermani assembled a final copy of the manuscript, he photocopied this page and placed it back in chronological order, indicating clearly that the text on the top of the page and the added text on the

---

35. John Ashbery, correspondence with Mark Ford, 2012. Courtesy of the Estate of John Ashbery.

36. A selection of Ashbery's correspondence with Ford from 1986–2017, along with a list of these names, was edited by Ford and published in *PN Review* 44.3 (Jan./Feb. 2018).

bottom from November 9 and 13, 2002, belong to separate sections. The text from November 13 spills over onto another typescript page. This discrepancy in the typescripts makes some sense, given that it corresponds with Ashbery's trip to France and the UK in 2002, and marks a return to the poem after a nearly three-month hiatus. "21 Variations on My Room" was written during this break. This is a prime example of a place where Kermani's careful notetaking was essential to reordering the poem.

164: "*New factors entered in.*"

See the seventh line of section 16 in "21 Variations on My Room," "New factors have entered the equation."[37]

164–65: "*Mostly it's the getting back, a chore like a sea wind and gulls coming to meet you, you'd hoped for more than this, or more comfort at least, but it's always a 'gray area.'*"

The original typescript reads "Mistly it's the *getting back*"; there is a chance Ashbery intended this word, as it is in keeping with the atmosphere of the "sea wind," but given that "i" and "o" are in such close proximity on the keyboard, and after conferring with Kermani and several other trusted colleagues, I have supplied the likelier "mostly."

165: "*Oh, we're not floating at all. We're partial home buyers and as such spend a lot of time on the floor, just lolling. We sat on it and jerked it. In the fullness of time a foolish man did a good thing.*"

The section beginning with this passage, written November 13, 2002, begins on its own page, but is connected to the previous three sentences after Ashbery's November 9 entry on the previous page, which Ashbery erroneously typed underneath a copy of entries from June 4 and June 5 (see entry for p. **141**, "My Own Best Customer"). Kermani made note of this connection on a photocopy of the original typescript, observing that there is mention of a "floor" in the entry on the previous typescript page ("We can go back to being in the order

---

37. *Parallel Movement of the Hands*, 104.

of each other's beds, and the rugs beside them, and the chairs pushed against the bed to make a kind of steps leading to the floor—"), which links the entries narratively. There is no indication of whether Ashbery wanted a paragraph break between this and the previous entry, but I have inserted one, as it seems appropriate.

The phrases "Oh, we're not floating at all" and "We sat on it and jerked it" appear earlier in the brief, lineated passage of "My Own Best Customer."[38] The phrase "In the fullness of time a foolish man did a good thing" appears toward the end of "A Lost Dog."[39]

165: "Think Fast, Mr. Moto."

The first in an eight-film series of Mr. Moto detective films (1937 1939) starring Peter Lorre and directed by Norman Foster.

165: *"The prancing of tires on a frozen roadway, expecting to promise what we knew no random event could deliver."*

Ashbery wrote "even" where I have supplied "event." "Even" is, perhaps, an archaic usage for "evening," but far likelier is that he accidentally omitted the "t."

[untitled] "Nothing if found convenient." (166)

Ashbery indicated that he wanted a "break" here. This and the next page are the only instances in the typescript's final pages where he specifies breaks. He types "KRP break 13" at the top of the page, later crossing out the "13" and replacing it with a "22." Though it's unclear as to whether he meant paragraph break or section break, I have inserted a section break, since there is a large amount of space at the bottom of the previous page/section.

166: *"That boy who looked adoringly at you twenty, thirty or forty years ago, with the gentle Kane Richmond eyes and licorice breath"*

---

38. *Parallel Movement of the Hands*, 143.

39. Ibid., 141.

In Ashbery's printed source material, Grant Tracey begins his article on *Spy Smasher*, "In chapter three, 'Iron Coffin,' Witney cues us to expect the unexpected. He constructs a typical sequence: Spy Smasher busts into a warehouse; a licorice trail of gun powder blazes."[40]

There You Go! (167)

Two chapters before, the phrase "there you go" appears as the second sentence of "[untitled] Are you trying to stop us?"[41]

167: *"All about you would be milling and streaming, rivers of Roman striped ribbons from cartwheel hats that say, 'No, excuse us! Please, you be the guest.'"*

Ashbery omitted end quotation marks, so I have made an educated guess as to where to place them.

167: *"'Shucks, I was, but I guess I'll stay now, or maybe I'll go, it's kind of getting to be time . . .'"*

I added the open quotation marks to this bit of dialogue.

169: *"Surely this is the reason we are all drawn to art, and why art loves us, and if anything were any different, that is more or less perfect, it wouldn't have the same hold over us."*

Given the position of letters on the keyboard and the context of this sentence, I interpreted the word that Ashbery typed as "efe" as "were."

[untitled] "Why wait for another day to cross itself?" (170)

Ashbery began this section on its own page (erroneously labeled "KRP 15") on

---

40. Grant Tracey, "Cliffhangers: Spy Smasher," *Images*, 4, www.imagesjournal.com /issue04/infocus/spysmasher.htm.

41. *Parallel Movement of the Hands*, 164.

November 24, 2002; the page also contains entries from November 25 and December 2 (the latter of which spills over onto the next page). On November 25, the ribbon ran out of ink, resulting in a very faint area of text ("They never bother to check those things. . . . Rejoice in the thousands of cousins that support you, and after that never say the dark cart isn't coming to get you."). The ribbon was replaced in the middle of the entry. This page was then retyped on a computer by either Kermani or (likelier) Marcella Durand, Ashbery's assistant at the time, who mentioned "typ[ing] in The Kane Richmond Project" in a note she saved to the office laptop in NYC. The previous section, "There You Go!" ends in the middle of the previous page, and it is unclear whether or not this page is a continuation of that section. Here, I have inserted a section break and treated the text as a separate, untitled chapter.

171: *"It may happen then as it has in the past that the spider king will unhitch himself to plummet directly into our daily affairs as they seemed on the point of opening, creating themselves and us as a by-product?"*

Here the original text reads "ot hopening," so Ashbery may have intended either "of opening" or "of happening."

172–73: *"The villains have Kane trapped in a barn and are starting to set fire to it. Then it's all over, for this week at least. The feature is beginning and the music wells up very lively and somber; it's a romance starring that lovely Greta Gynt. Pass me a mint, dear. I'm afraid my mascara is streaked. It must look awful in this rapid play of flashing lights and shadows. Heavens! It seems the projector is broken. We'll have to wait in the dark. Only they've turned the lights up now. Somebody is going to make some kind of announcement."*

This passage is full of interesting details. Though we have glimpsed him many times, Kane Richmond (the actor) is "introduced." As readers and viewers, we are placed before a feature film in the movie theater, the site where one would have experienced these serials. We pass through a cliffhanger moment (the one relayed here is the ending scene from chapter 3 of *The Adventures of Rex and Rinty*) into the moving opening credits of a film starring Norwegian actress

Greta Gynt, perhaps *Mr. Emmanuel* (1944), which is indeed a romance with "lively and somber" music accompanying its opening credits. Finally, we are thrown into the abstract flashes of a mechanical failure. The projector has broken.

An Unspecified Amount (174)

Ashbery handwrote the first draft of this section, in part, along with what became "*très modéré*," on two pages (legal pad, undated), and later typed it under the section "Arguably," with no chapter title to separate it. On the first page of the handwritten draft, he titled the section "An Unspecified Amount,"[42] which he did not carry over to the typescript. On the second page of the handwritten draft, he wrote "Fried Mackerel and Frozen Peas" in the margin,[43] which became the title of the chapter following "*très modéré*." I have reinstated "An Unspecified Amount" in the interest of seriality and in case it was omitted in error.

Kermani noted on photocopies of the handwritten pages that this text becomes the December 4, 7, and 10, 2002, entries in the typescript, and that the original handwritten pages were missing. He found them on June 10, 2003, almost a month after he first assembled the final copy.

174: *"Someone must have been telling lies about John A."*
This line echoes the opening of Franz Kafka's *The Trial* (1925): "Someone must have been telling lies about Josef K."

174: *"Even then he could survey the street through a species of panopticon he had rigged up, which he liked to say was better than television, since it was free and never required adjustment."*
On several occasions while I was working for him, Ashbery enlisted my assistance in remembering the word "panopticon."

---

42. See fig. 11.
43. See fig. 12.

174: *"One day a Fuller Brush man happened by,"*

A "Fuller Brush man" was a door-to-door salesman of personal and household products from the Fuller Brush Company. This occupation was dramatized in the comedic film *The Fuller Brush Man* (1948), starring Red Skelton and directed by S. Sylvan Simon. A Fuller Brush man also makes an appearance in Ashbery's prose poem "Be Careful What You Wish For," published in his collection *Breezeway* (2015): "Go back to sleep. And they did (writing in the grass). The Fuller Brush man (clean-jawed) stopped by. See you down there. Lemme know. Just because Scooby Doo thinks you should . . ."[44]

très modéré (175)

175: *"he had just unwittingly opened new avenues in a conversation in a conversation that was fast becoming vexatious."*

I did not correct the doubling of "in a conversation," as Ashbery may have intended it to underline the exasperating nature of the conversation between the characters. The repetition also recalls Ashbery's poem "A Sweet Disorder": "It can't have escaped your escaped your attention / that I would argue. / How was it supposed to look? / Do I wake or sleep?"[45]

Fried Mackerel and Frozen Peas (176)

I have adhered to Ashbery's unique formatting in the verse portion of this chapter as much as possible, treating the last segment of this section as "broken prose," wherein I follow paragraph breaks strictly, but line breaks may differ from the original, in order to prioritize Ashbery's unique, mid-sentence breaks within long lines. The text of this section reaches the bottom of the typescript page.

---

44. Ashbery, *Breezeway*, 104.

45. Ibid., 105.

[untitled] "*The point is to find an*
extra-sensual way to be without it." (177)

This final passage of *The Kane Richmond Project* begins on its own page but, as is typical in this portion of the typescript, Ashbery gave no indication as to whether or not there is a section break or paragraph break in between this and the previous section, or whether this entry is part of "Fried Mackerel and Frozen Peas" at all. So I have deferred to Ashbery's sense of a false ending or cliffhanger at the end of "Fried Mackerel and Frozen Peas" on the previous typescript page. He writes, "There's lots of new openings. And the air, the air is rife with possibilities. Just don't tell anybody I told you about it. That would be the end, friend, the end." Here I chose to take a formal cue from Ashbery's content. Breaking the section allows for a second ending that is very much a "new opening."

ACKNOWLEDGMENTS

The Estate of John Ashbery gratefully acknowledges the following publications in which poems and excerpts from *Parallel Movement of the Hands* first appeared, sometimes in slightly different forms: *Conjunctions, Image, jubilat, The New York Review of Books, The Paris Review,* and *Poetry London.*

* * *

This book was, in many ways, a collaborative effort. In his preface to *Other Traditions*, Ashbery discusses his difficulty with preparing his Charles Eliot Norton lectures for publication, writing:

> The main problem was that of transforming a lecture into an essay, the spoken language and the written one being subtly at odds with one another. It may have been harder for me since the spoken language is the one I use when I write poetry. Luckily I have a friend who is a superb poet as well as a former book editor and now a professor of literature at the United States Merchant Marine Academy, where she runs a tight ship. Rosanne Wasserman ... has been of immense help to me, typing and editing my manuscript and tracking down elusive references, as has her husband Eugene Richie.[1]

Thankfully, the "friend and superb poet" Ashbery mentions, Rosanne Wasserman, is also *my* friend, and her emotional as well as practical guidance during this process, along with that of her husband, Eugene Richie, has been invaluable. This was my first foray into preparing original manuscript materials for publication. Often when I came to Wasserman with a query that I thought was perhaps an error, she was able to uncover Ashbery's "spoken language," locating his voice, or a voice he was momentarily inhabiting, such as the unique upstate New York

---

1. John Ashbery, preface to *Other Traditions*. Harvard University Press, 2000.

speech patterns in which Ashbery was saturated during his youth. I was truly lucky to have her as an advisor on this project.

I am also inexpressibly grateful to Ashbery's husband, David Kermani, to whom this publication is dedicated. Kermani has been a part of this book since its inception, and without his meticulous annotation and organization of Ashbery's papers, as well as his guidance and constant support, these works would not have been published. While I worked for Ashbery, it was beautiful to witness Kermani's care for Ashbery and his work, the ways he developed conversations surrounding Ashbery's poetry that extended toward other art forms and disciplines. He is the founder of the Ashbery Resource Center, a searchable online archive of Ashbery-related materials curated and maintained by the Flow Chart Foundation, which I utilized throughout my research; it is an essential and growing resource for anyone interested in Ashbery's influence, influences, and legacy.

The poet and translator Marcella Durand, Ashbery's assistant from 2002 to 2007, has been a steadfast advisor on this book and played the special role of recommending me for the position of Ashbery's assistant. Ben Lerner's commitment and contributions to the project from its early stages have been bolstering and inspiring. Karin Roffman, Ashbery's biographer, was a consistent source of insight, both in person and in her written scholarship. I am grateful for the scholarship of poet Mark Ford, Ashbery's dear friend, and editor of his collected volumes with Library of America. And, as I have already declared, I am indebted to the editorial companionship of my—and Ashbery's—friend, Farnoosh Fathi.

For their longtime support of Ashbery's writing and career, and for their belief in this book, thank you to Georges Borchardt, Dan Halpern, Gabriella Doob, and the entire Ecco staff. For his continued visual relationship to Ashbery's books and poetry, thank you to designer Jeff Clark.

For her essential work formatting and copyediting the appendices, thanks to Michelle Martinez. Ashbery's Hudson assistants, Mark Allen and Timothy O'Connor, were incredibly helpful, as was Alisa Goz, whose detailed cataloging of Ashbery's music collections in Hudson and NYC allowed me to track down specific Czerny recordings. Michael Dumanis, Mark Bibbins, and Matt Walker were kind to help me find elusive page numbers while I was separated from my books. I am also grateful to Sandy Noble, who took beautiful photographs of some of the source materials that Ashbery collaged and referenced in *The Kane Richmond Project*.

Though I was ultimately unable to make my scheduled visit to Ashbery's archive at Harvard University due to the widespread closures caused by the COVID-19 pandemic, I am very grateful for the help and guidance of Leslie Morris, Gore Vidal Curator of Modern Books and Manuscripts at Houghton Library, and her colleague, Assistant Curator Christine Jacobson.

I transcribed "The History of Photography" while on residency at the T. S. Eliot House in Gloucester, Massachusetts, and am grateful to the director, Dana Hawkes, for her hospitality, kindness, delicious cooking, and conversation.

Some concepts and quotes from my introduction regarding Ashbery's relationship to film first appeared in my interview of filmmaker Michael Almereyda for the Criterion Collection website. Special thanks are due to Almereyda for his support of this project.

For conversations and correspondence about Ashbery, his poetry and process, that shaped this collection, I thank Adam Fitzgerald, John Yau, Shane McCrae, Guy Maddin, Hans Ulrich Obrist, Richard Deming, Dara Wier, David Gorin, Jeffrey Lependorf, and Kamran Javadizadeh.

Thank you to Eric Dean Wilson, Zachary Pace, and Andrew Epstein for their vital feedback on early drafts of my introduction; and to Ali Power, Samantha Zighelboim, Mia Kang, Simone Kearney, Barbara Heller, Timothy Donnelly, Dorothea Lasky, Rachel Levitsky, Ana Paula Simões, Krystal Languell, Ava Lehrer, Katie Raissian, Gregory Scheidler, Todd Colby, Alan Felsenthal, Chia-Lun Chang, Daniel Poppick, Gabrielle Lind, Milla Bell-Hart, Casey Llewellyn, and Claudia Rankine for their encouragement, advice, and friendship.

Thank you to Patricia and Philip Kennedy-Grant for their gift of shelter and care in the early days of the pandemic, during which I edited much of this book. And to my partner, Alex Kennedy-Grant, for his endless patience and calm presence.

Finally, thanks to my unbelievably supportive and loving parents, Lois and Jim Skillings.

JOHN ASHBERY was born in Rochester, New York, in 1927. He earned degrees from Harvard and Columbia, and went to France as a Fulbright Scholar in 1955, living there for much of the next decade. His many collections of poetry include *Commotion of the Birds* (2016), *Breezeway* (2015), *Quick Question* (2012), *Planisphere* (2009), and *Notes from the Air: Selected Later Poems* (2007), which was awarded the 2008 International Griffin Poetry Prize. *Self-Portrait in a Convex Mirror* (1975) won the three major American prizes—the Pulitzer Prize, the National Book Award, and the National Book Critics Circle Award—and the early book *Some Trees* (1956) was selected by W. H. Auden for the Yale Younger Poets Series. The Library of America published two volumes of his collected poems (*1956–1987* in 2008 and *1991–2000* in 2017), and Ashbery was the first living poet to be included in the series. A two-volume set of his translations from the French (poetry and prose) was published in 2014. Active in various areas of the arts throughout his career, he served as executive editor of *ARTnews* and as art critic for *New York* magazine and *Newsweek*. He had several exhibitions of his collages at Tibor de Nagy Gallery, which represents his estate, and a book of his collages with a selection of his poems was published by Rizzoli in 2018. Ashbery taught for many years at Brooklyn College (CUNY) and Bard College, and from 1989 to 1990 delivered the Charles Eliot Norton lectures at Harvard, published as *Other Traditions* (2000). He was a member of the American Academy of Arts and Letters (receiving its Gold Medal for Poetry in 1977) and the American Academy of Arts and Sciences, and was a chancellor of the Academy of American Poets from 1988 to 1999. The winner of many prizes and awards both nationally and internationally, he received two Guggenheim Fellowships and was a MacArthur Fellow from 1985 to 1990. He was awarded the Medal for Distinguished Contribution to American Letters from the National Book Foundation (2011) and a National Humanities Medal, presented by President Barack

Obama at the White House (2012). His work has been translated into more than twenty-five languages. He collaborated with filmmakers, composers, visual artists, and writers. Ashbery died in September 2017 at the age of ninety. His work continues to inspire countless creative artists in many fields. Additional information is available in the "About John Ashbery" section of the Ashbery Resource Center's website, a project of the Flow Chart Foundation, www.flow chartfoundation.org/arc.

BEN LERNER is the author of seven books of poetry and prose. His most recent book is the novel *The Topeka School* (2019), which was a finalist for the Pulitzer Prize. The recipient of fellowships from the Fulbright, Guggenheim, and MacArthur foundations, he is a Distinguished Professor of English at Brooklyn College.

EMILY SKILLINGS is the author of the poetry collection *Fort Not* (2017), which *Publishers Weekly* called a "fabulously eccentric, hypnotic, and hypervigilant debut." She is a member of the Belladonna* Collaborative, a feminist poetry collective, small press, and event series in Brooklyn. She received her MFA from Columbia University School of the Arts, where she was a Creative Writing Teaching Fellow. Skillings was John Ashbery's assistant from 2010 to 2017.